A Million Shillings
Escape from Somalia

T0372282

Alixandra Fazzina

* * T R O L L E Y * *

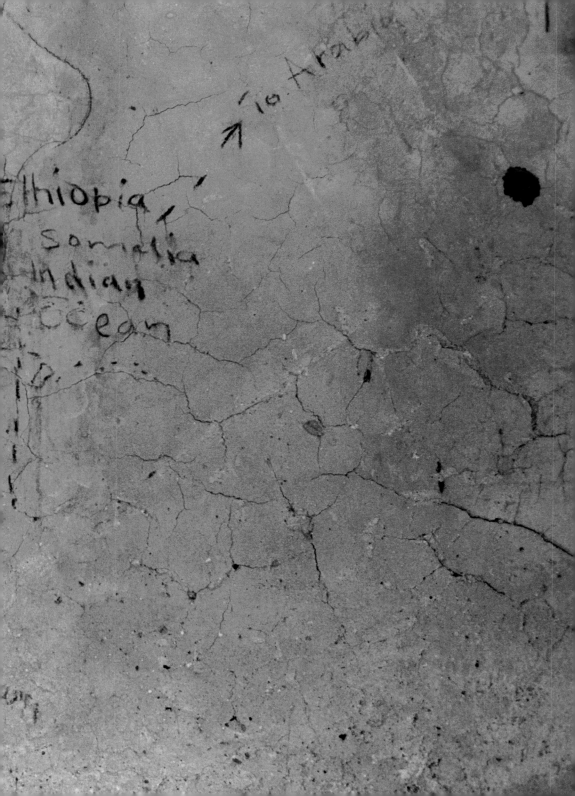

Previous pages
Mould slowly creeps over a crudely drawn map sketched
in charcoal, depicting smuggling routes from the Horn
of Africa "To Arabia", on the walls of an old fort close to
Somalia's southern frontier.

A Migration Poem

Oh ! My fellow countrymen

Observe thy people

They take a risky journey

Across The Gulf of Aden

Many have been told about the danger ahead

Determined in their choices

They choose to live or die

Rather than stay in a country

And see it as a hell

They pay for their lives in a small boat

With more than a hundred crowded

And callous men riding.

Ahmad Mohamed - Somali refugee, Al-Kahraz Camp, Yemen

SUDAN

SAUDI ARABIA

YEMEN

ERITREA
Asmara

Sana'a

Mukalla

Mayfa'Ah
Burum
Mayfa'ah Hagar
Bir Ali

Dhubab
Bisatine
Al-Kharaz
Aden

Ahwar

Obock

DJIBOUTI
Djibouti
Ali-Addeh

Bossaso

SOMALILAND

Jijiga

Hargeysa

PUNTLAND

Addis Ababa

Garoowe

ETHIOPIA

OGADEN

Galkayo

OROMIA

Belet Weyne

SOMALIA

Afgooye
Mogadishu

KENYA

Dadaab

Nairobi

GULF OF ADEN:
PEOPLE SMUGGLING AND
MIGRATION ROUTES

0   175   350

kilometres

Contents

Foreword

This is an astonishingly powerful book. More than any report my organization could prepare or any speech I could give, it tells the story of the thousands of people who risk their lives to cross the Gulf of Aden in search of safety and a better life. The author, Alixandra Fazzina, has achieved something remarkable – portraits which are intimate without being invasive and deeply sympathetic without being exploitative. I defy anyone to be unmoved by the photographs and stories in this book.

I recall well Ms. Fazzina's photographs, which UNHCR was privileged to use at its May 2008 regional conference in Sana'a on refugee protection and international migration, convened in cooperation with IOM and the other organizations of the Mixed Migration Taskforce for Somalia and hosted by the Government of Yemen. A number of the photographs are reproduced in this book, many now with the benefit of details about the individuals pictured.

Acknowledging that UNHCR does not have and does not seek a mandate for migration, I urged more than anything else in my remarks at the conference in Yemen the need for a coordinated, rights-based and humanitarian approach to the people who, often destitute of any other choice, risk their lives to get there.

Towards this end, very considerable progress has been made. The Government of Yemen has established a National Committee for Refugee Affairs (NACRA) which together with UNHCR and its implementing partners more systematically search for, receive and assist people arriving on Yemen's shores. Three permanent registration centres have been established by the Government of Yemen for Somali refugees. UNHCR meanwhile has increased the value of the assistance it provides in Yemen from USD 6.8 million in 2007 to USD 32.7 million in 2009.

There have also been significant changes in the number, composition and routing of people fleeing the Horn of Africa since the time the photographs were taken. The estimated total number of migrants and refugees arriving on Yemen's shores in 2006 was 22,000. In 2007, it was 29,000. In 2008, it almost doubled, to more than 50,000.

In 2009, it increased by more than half again, to over 77,000.

While the movement continues to be almost entirely composed of Somalis and Ethiopians, the proportions have reversed - from two thirds being Somali to two thirds being Ethiopian. This does not mean there has been an improvement in the situation in Somalia - indeed the situation has deteriorated markedly in the last two years - but rather that more Ethiopians are making the voyage.

This has increased the attractiveness of other migration routes, both across the Red Sea rather than the Gulf of Aden and southwards to other parts of the African continent. While the increased use of the Red Sea reflects a continuing sense of desperation on the part of Ethiopians risking the voyage, most of whom are migrants rather than refugees, there is a significant upside in the change of routes – the substantially shorter crossing has reduced the number of known and suspected deaths en route tenfold, from one in twenty to one in two hundred.

What has not changed is the conspicuous and thoroughly gratuitous brutality towards the migrants and refugees making the trip. Whether driven by drug-induced stupefaction, a desire to demonstrate their obviously if invidiously greater power or sheer habit, smugglers continue to tie up, burn, butt end, suffocate, shoot and throw overboard their charges. A million shillings is not enough to buy decent treatment for the voyagers but it is enough to sustain impunity for the perpetrators of wholly unnecessary brutality.

Yemen has been and remains exceptionally generous to the Somalis arriving on its shores. It continues to provide refugee status and thus protection against return to Somalia on a prima facie (or presumptive) basis. Recognizing that some of the Ethiopians arriving also have international protection concerns, it has recently allowed UNHCR and NACRA to screen arrivals.

These are policies worthy not only of commendation but support. To put it in perspective, based on the total number of Somalis arriving and just the approximately seven per cent of Ethiopians who seek asylum after arriving, Yemen received last year three quarters as many asylum-seekers as the United States – and the United States received more asylum claims in 2009 than any other industrialized country. Yemen's generosity comes despite the mounting challenges the country faces and should not be presumed inexhaustible.

This is even more important today with the impact of the global economic downturn on the economies and attitudes towards migrants in the Gulf. For Saudi Arabia, the destination of so many of the people profiled in this book, both the willing migrant and unwilling victim of trafficking, the situation has been further complicated by the recent Al Houthi rebellion in northern Yemen, which provoked a cross-border response by Saudi forces and significant reinforcement of the border.

As a result, more of the people arriving in Yemen may seek or be required to remain there. For those entitled to remain, more support will be required for self-reliance and livelihoods activities, particularly in the urban centres to which migrants and refugees continue to gravitate, but also for resettlement. For those not entitled to remain in Yemen and willing to return, as many of the Ethiopian migrants are, we must ensure their repatriation in safety and dignity, ideally with assistance to help them reintegrate where they have come from, free from crippling shame or debt. At the regional level, we need to expand the humanitarian support available in the Horn, particularly in Somalia, and to continue to explore legal migration options so people are not driven to risk their lives in order to improve them.

These things have to be more than exhortations or hopes. The people in this book need more than words. The woman whose baby - born on the smugglers' boat - was thrown overboard; the woman mistaken for dead and nearly buried alive; the man beaten so severely he may never become self-supporting; the orphaned daughter of a woman forced into survival sex; the pre-pubescent children who fled from forced recruitment and made their way alone to Yemen from Mogadishu – if ever on earth people needed our solidarity, these are the people, the people of this book.

António Guterres
United Nations High Commissioner for Refugees, Geneva, May 2010

Mogadishu Road

"Radio Kabila! Come in. Repeat. This is Radio Kabila!"

In a tiny office in downtown Bossaso named after Congo's president, a CB radio operator, locked behind a wire cage, shouts at his crackling apparatus. The walls are covered in graffiti depicting skull and crossbones, US dollars, a Somali flag, mobile phone numbers and the words, "Tsunami is disaster, is punishment." It is a hawala bureau, one of hundreds that operate around the largest port town in the Horn of Africa and the radio operator is trying to make contact with a truck driver on the Mogadishu Road carrying people. As just one tiny link in Somalia's human trafficking business, Radio Kabila is going to take their money.

As civil war in Somalia draws on into its second decade, the country lies in ruins and remains without effective government. Once an Italian idyll on the Indian Ocean where expatriates ate locally produced pasta, roamed freely around the bazaars and danced in beachside nightclubs, its capital city Mogadishu has become almost depopulated. Fought over by warlords and more recently by young, unpredictable and heavily armed fighters of the Shabaab militias, successive peacekeeping missions have done little to protect the impoverished citizens or bolster proxy regimes. Daily rocket attacks and street-to-street fighting have left almost every family broken. Homes and loved ones have been devastated amid this ruined, bullet-scarred city. Nearly everyone wants to find a way out, worn down by the gunfire and death.

The least risky escape from Mogadishu is along a corridor running inland to the wells of Afgooye. However there is little water for the hundreds of thousands of displaced who have sought refuge in the camps. Improvised shelters of tree branches covered in unpicked clothes and sheets line a twenty kilometre stretch of road. Uncertain security allows for only a trickle of aid to get through and attacks have forced out many NGOs providing assistance. Afgooye is a grim retreat.

Long established camps on Kenya's border that are home to more than a quarter of a million Somalis are no better option. Severe overcrowding and serious shortages of food, water and shelter have seen refugees turning around, preferring to confront the risks of conflict at home rather than persevere among these ragged mini-cities in the desert. Deep-rooted clan politics make the camps in the more stable Somaliland region an unwelcoming alternative to residents of south-central Somalia, and with ongoing conflicts spanning the Ethiopian frontiers, the dispossessed find themselves literally hemmed in.

Desperate and in fear for their lives, there is one other feasible means of escape from this beleaguered country. With the longest coastline in Africa, tens of thousands each year turn to the sea. Yemen has become the obvious haven but the long land and sea journey there can be perilous, and in many cases fatal. In a country obsessed with getting its news from the radio, stories and public information campaigns mean that most people are well aware of the route and its inherent dangers. Afraid that they will lose their lives if they stay at home and too scared to open their front doors to go out for food, few however stop to weigh-up the risks.

Agents from smuggling networks lure the young and vulnerable from the outset. Strategically placed offices across the southern regions entice those wishing to escape with all-inclusive packages and promises of a better life. Not everyone uses their services at this stage but most will be happy to hear false reassurances and readily take-up contacts for the road ahead.

Uprooting themselves from homes and families they will never return to, the would-be voyagers carry little with them. Littered with checkpoints run by the warlords and their militias, Somalia's lawless roads are notorious for banditry. Travelling north on trucks and buses, passengers carry only a few clothes and some spare shillings to pay for meals or buy off violent threats at roadblocks en route. War widows and single women are frequently dragged from vehicles at gunpoint only to be raped in full view of defenceless onlookers, while men are often beaten and robbed for loose change, cigarettes or a mobile phone. Just leaving their towns and villages can be fraught with danger.

Some make the journey in stages, picking up casual work as they go. A few days spent labouring or breaking rocks can buy the next fare. The majority head directly to the fractious town of Galkayo, some seven hundred and fifty kilometres north of Mogadishu. Situated on the border of the semi-autonomous state of Puntland and split by an ethnic divide, all transport coming from the south must stop short of what is an invisible green line. Violent clan battles often erupt here, scattering IDPs who have sought sanctuary in encampments that fill patches of wasteland between abandoned houses, considered too dangerous for anybody to call home anymore. Transiting on foot to the far transport terminals, many spend days or weeks in northern Galkayo while they wait for extra funds to be sent. Others are simply exhausted after hours spent held up at checkpoints and on Somalia's dilapidated roads. They bed down for a while in clandestine halfway houses hidden away behind scruffy bus stops or cafes, or else impose on displaced families.

Once in Puntland, those on their way to Yemen are joined by Ethiopian migrants and refugees escaping hardship, conflict and human rights abuses across the border. Together with the wayfaring Somalis, they are often quickly approached by middlemen who work the hubs and doss houses of Galkayo, touting on behalf of the smuggling gangs. Offering to arrange onward transport, a place to stay in Bossaso and assuring safe passage on the voyage across the Gulf of Aden, these brokers are adept at engaging the steady flow of potential human cargo and securing allegiances to the syndicates they promote.

Once groups of migrants and refugees have been collected together, they are packed tightly into trucks or mini vans ahead of the final leg of their journey through Somalia. Back on the main Mogadishu highway, they continue north along straight and seemingly never-ending roads. Passing through Puntland's capital Garoowe, they spend hours hunched up, as the approach to Africa's Horn traverses featureless plains, with the hot sun and biting wind making the already uncomfortable ride feel tortuous. Then, upon nearing Bossaso, the drivers call ahead to offices such as Radio Kabila; at the end of the road the smugglers will be waiting.

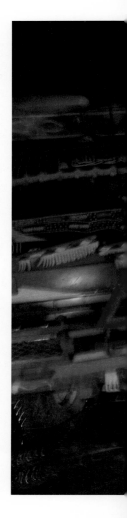

Situated on Somalia's main north south highway, the colloquially named
"Moqdishu Restaurant" is one of the first stopping-off points for migrants
and refugees heading north from the capital, on their way across the Gulf of
Aden to Yemen. Open late into the night, displaced teenage boys at the busy
café dish up food and drink, while a clandestine smuggler's bureau and doss
house to the rear facilitate new arrivals.

People pick their way through the muddy, dimly lit streets around Bossaso town at night after heavy rains.

After dark, herds of goats pass by destroyed buildings at an intersection outside Bossaso's port gates. For the thousands of migrants and refugees passing through this transit hub on their way to Yemen each year, approaching the town's seafront is a sign that they have finally reached the end point of their journey in Somalia.

Travelling for seemingly endless miles through the featureless stony plains that typify the landscape north of Galkayo, distant hazy mountains and rows of shacks signify the beginnings of Bossaso, and the end of the Mogadishu road.

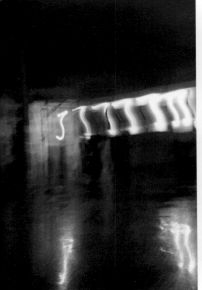

Having been dropped off on the roadside in Bossaso, a smuggler's agent coordinates
the latest new arrivals from Mogadishu, as they are transferred into a small bus that will
transport them to a covert halfway house in the town.

Heading back to a smuggler's house on the periphery of one of the many
sprawling refugee camps, a man walks quickly along a dusty road on the edge
of Bossaso town at dusk. At night, the back streets and camps of Bossaso
become dangerous places in which to hang around, due to continued clan
violence and the risk of robbery from armed gangs who prey on new arrivals.

Clouded by the fumes of burning plastic, a muddy patch of wasteland on the Mogadishu Road is
the main dropping off point for passengers arriving from Somalia's south. Trucks and small buses
converge on the site located a few kilometres outside Bossaso town. From here, the only routes
ahead are the small stony tracks that hug Puntland's coast.
As they climb down from overloaded trucks, many of the travellers are met by smugglers
who quickly whisk them away to hidden halfway houses dotting the slums and camps of this
supposed coastal haven. Disorientated after such a long journey, others easily fall prey to the
exploitative middlemen of gangs, or thieves offering would-be advice, only to rob the new
arrivals of the little money or possessions they have on their way into town.

34

Above and following pages
Working for a people trafficking syndicate, a CB radio operator talks to truck drivers bringing migrants and refugees along the Mogadishu Road to Bossaso. Known as "Radio Kabila" after Congo's president, this Hawiye smuggling gang's Bossaso office is linked to a chain of others across south central Somalia. Sitting behind a fenced off desk, the operator slowly attends to a row of customers that have been sitting on plastic chairs under a painted skull and cross-bones since early morning. On their way to Yemen, they are waiting for hawala money transfers to arrive from relatives; few have carried enough cash for their onward sea journey fearing robbery on the roads. Their families will have to visit a sister office to send the money and it cannot be paid out here until the operator receives a call on the radio. Once it comes, it is unlikely that it will ever leave Radio Kabila. Most will immediately pay the fare of a million shillings to the boss in order to secure their passage across the Gulf of Aden. For now though they must be patient; the agent is busy talking to middlemen as they coordinate a pick-up of the latest batch of potential customers due to arrive in town any moment.

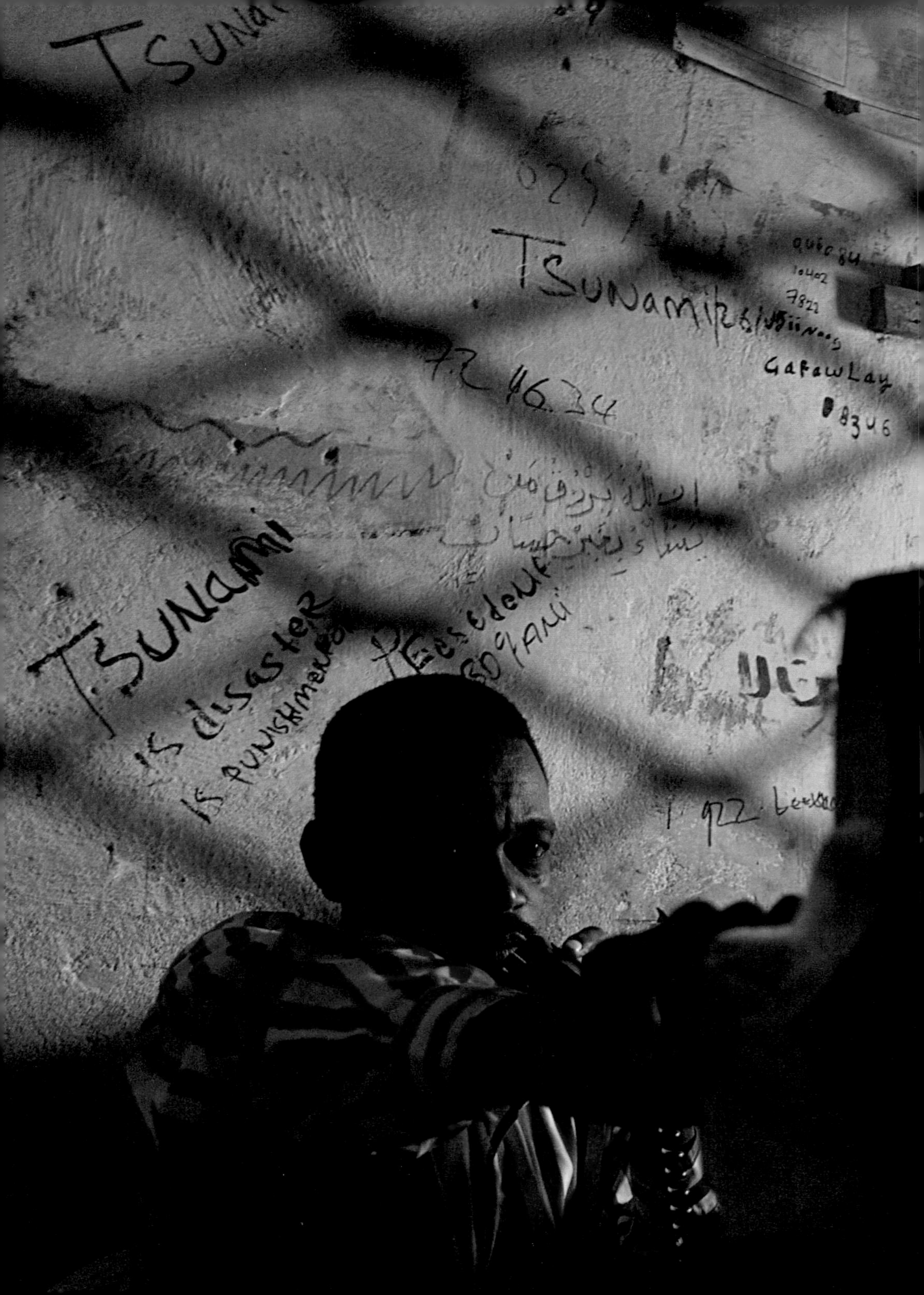
TSUNAMI
TSUNAMI
IS disaster
GafawLay

We Are Tahrib

In Somalia they have a word for illegal emigrants - *tahrib*. In Bossaso thousands arrive each week. The town is notorious as one of the world's biggest hubs for people smuggling and trafficking. Serving as the major transit centre for the refugees and migrants heading across the Gulf of Aden to Yemen and the Arabian Peninsula, the tahrib fuel the economy in what is the biggest grossing industry here.

In its heyday Bossaso was a thriving fishing centre, where life revolved around the arrival of wooden dhows importing goods from across the Indian Ocean. Now surrounded by derelict ice factories and processing plants, only a few fishermen supply a tiny seafood market on the town's debris-strewn beach, while a couple of boats a day offload Coca-Cola and cheap packaged food stuffs. The investment opportunities that exist today are in the call centres, money transfer offices, cafes, laundries and halfway houses that serve the burgeoning people smuggling business. From armed guards to guesthouse owners, to drivers and tea sellers, money from the desperate refugees and migrants sustains almost the entire local population. As the numbers of tahrib transiting through Bossaso rises year after year, the gang leaders and boat owners grow richer. They have become the town's "big fish".

Relatively stable compared to south-central Somalia, Bossaso is seen by outsiders in the region as a tranquil coastal haven where life is good and the streets are paved with gold. Many come here hoping to find work and an easy life by the sea but their dreams are quickly shattered. Surrounding the town's dusty unpaved bazaars, tattered camps sprawl in all directions out into the dry desert plains. Looking for refuge, the displaced find that their only sanctuaries are at the end of stony paths, where they are often forced to sit in the harsh sea winds and literally unpick the clothes they have with them in order to fashion crude shelters.

The scene in these afflicted settlements changes little; children walk barefoot through mounting piles of rubbish and human waste while women scavenge for anything they can use to cook their next meal on. Rates of malnutrition and disease are high, and when aid does sporadically reach the impoverished, the sound of gunfire often signals that it has been looted from the intended recipients by merciless bandits.

Most of the residents had planned only to pass through, stopping long enough to earn themselves some money and then continue onwards to a "better life" in Yemen. The reality is that many become trapped in these vast settlements of weather beaten tents, far from home and penniless. Like the endless stream of new arrivals, their dreams lie across the water.

Amongst the homemade tents, newly arrived tahrib find shelter in the ironically named "safe houses", operated by middlemen and women working on behalf of the smuggling gangs. Often segregated ethnically, the travellers pay a little rent to sleep on overcrowded floors under cardboard or plastic sheeting, concealed amid the debris of the bush camps. Others are located in so-called boli houses, hidden away in the town's narrow back alleys. Here conditions are a little better but savings are quickly eroded by unanticipated food and accommodation costs.

Huge numbers of migrants and refugees arrive in Bossaso without either contacts or the means to survive. They are drawn to the port area in a usually fruitless search for work. By night the streets and disused storage depots here are lined with rows of bodies bedding down in the open air. Exposed to robbery and abuse, the single women and unaccompanied children among the sleepers cluster closely together in an often futile bid to protect themselves. With nowhere to go, and unsure of how they will proceed, such vulnerable individuals are susceptible to the agents of traffickers who lure them with offers of free travel and job opportunities across the gulf. Most are too desperate to ignore such invitations, and many will inevitably be led into a life of slavery.

Unlike the brief stopover they had imagined, life for the majority of tahrib in Bossaso is a waiting game. Most spend their days visiting call centres and hawala bureaus as they try to contact friends and relatives back home who have promised to send funds for their onward journey. Each must pay their chosen smuggling gang a million shillings - the equivalent of 50 US dollars - in order to secure their place on a boat to Yemen. In what is known as the "open season", on either side of the summer monsoons, weather conditions are better and smugglers ply the route on an almost daily basis. Still the high demand can lead to backlogs.

A single tiny vessel can carry upwards of one hundred and twenty passengers but the middlemen must first collect their charges together in precisely numbered groups before their leaders give the go ahead to leave. Even then the migrants and refugees may have to bide their time. Most of the tahrib spend a minimum of a week or two sitting out the days restlessly in their doss houses, anxious not to stray too far in case they miss the often sudden orders to proceed.

Waiting for the sea crossing that they have now staked their lives on, the days are passed dozing, drinking tea, chewing qat and watching old videos with no soundtrack. Packing and re-packing the few possessions that they have carried with them, the tahrib know that not all of them will survive the coming journey.

In the dry scrubland of Shebelle B's Camp #6, karate instructor Ahado spars with one of his pupils on a cleared patch of ground in front of his tent, that improvises as a martial arts school.

Fleeing threats of violence in Mogadishu, Ahado and his family made the long journey to Bossaso with the dream of setting sail in search of a new life. Unable to raise the money, Adaho became stuck, and so found a spot to pitch a shelter he constructed himself from sticks, sheets and cardboard boxes. Reaching the shores of Yemen remains in his thoughts each day, but for now, he makes a few shillings teaching afternoon classes of karate to other displaced Somalis in the surrounding camps. It keeps him feeling human.

From the stony approaches to the coastal desert, camps sprawl across the forsaken landscape around Bossaso town. Some have been there for nearly twenty years since the outbreak of civil war in Somalia; only the residents continue to change as the exodus of people continues. Named informally after different regions of the country, or simply referred to by numbers, Bush Camp #1 is just one of these squalid settlements. Shelters are crudely constructed of anything found - torn clothes and sheets, sticks, cardboard boxes, sacks and the shells of oil drums. Rain often soaks the residents through their flimsy weatherproofing, as plastic sheeting is hard to come by. Few have anything to sleep on or cover them at night to protect them from the strong winds. Distributions by aid agencies are not enough, and cannot reach everyone.

Sitting in her makeshift tent in the dusty Bulo Elay Camp, thirty two year old Hakumo Abdulahi looks down at her sick three month old son Ahmed in despair. Severely malnourished and suffering from a bout of bad diarrhea from drinking the unprotected local water, Ahmed has made little in the way of recovery. Despite Hakumo seeking assistance from a clinic run by the World Food Programme, she is worried that he won't pull through.

Escaping from Mogadishu a year ago with just the clothes on her back, Hakumo left her other children behind with a relative in order to follow her husband to Bossaso by truck; she discovered she was pregnant soon after. Originally planning to escape Somalia for the shores of Yemen, the family have now been forced to eke out a life in the camps of Bossaso, unable to return home or to continue their journey. Hakumo has no word as to whether her other children are alive or dead.

A newly arrived tahrib unrolls his bedding in the back room of a halfway house run by a smuggling gang near Bossaso port.

Having just been paid by a group of temporary residents, Mohamed Wardhi sits counting out a pile of Somali shillings in the makeshift café that he runs just outside Bossaso's port gates. One of ten or so such cafes serving up chai and Ethiopian coffee, in a dirty thoroughfare made up solely of orange tarpaulin-covered shelters, each serves as a mini transit centre for the thousands of Ethiopian migrants and refugees that pass through the town each year, as they escape deprivation and conflict in the Ogaden and Oromia. Acting as a go between for one of the smuggling gangs, Mohamed supplements his income by directing new arrivals to the appropriate henchmen, many of who frequent the surrounding establishments in search of their next batch of human cargo.

After 9pm, Mohamed's café transforms to become part of a street of clandestine doss houses, where the coffee drinkers of the day bed down for the night laid out in rows under the orange plastic, dreaming of Yemen. Each morning, Mohamed will collect a fee from them.

Right
A female migrant from Ethiopia sits beside a national airline bag as she rests in the shade at Mohamed Wardhi's cafe.

Following pages
Ethiopian refugee Zahara rests beside a cooking fire, in a makeshift camp hemmed into the walls behind Bossaso's port. After the long overland journey through Somalia, Zahara is now using a small café there as a base, as she waits to depart in smugglers' boats. Like many of the other tahrib in Bossaso, she is searching for a better life free from violence.
Smiling and laughing with a group of women she met on the way, Zahara eventually left Somalia a week later from a sandy beach under blue skies. Hitting a patch of bad weather at sea, the tiny boat in which she was travelling capsized as it began to take on water. Only eleven of the one hundred and forty passengers on board are known to have survived. Zahara is believed dead.

Jibril's orange-covered café sits just along the street from Mohamed's. There is little to tell them apart. Silent Amharic pop videos cast light from old television sets, young men sit playing cards at the tables built from sticks, while women braiding their hair can be seen hidden behind torn pieces of sheeting in a kind of disrupted purda. Thermos flasks of hot water sit ready for customers who have plenty of time to kill. Waiting for the boats can be restless and the tahrib have little to do to fill their time. Few have enough money even to afford a cheap hot meal from the women, usually sat cooking at a fire in the corner.

The customers haven't had to search hard for Jibril's place by the port - many have already been informed of its whereabouts by smuggling networks across the border in towns like Harar.

Over the years, the orange-covered café owners are branching out as they make some cash, investing in money exchange offices, telephone booths and boats - all to serve the tahrib, in what is Bossaso's biggest business.

When the sun comes up, residents at the Oromo Hotel pull up their scarves and blankets,
in order to hide their faces from the sun as they try to go back to sleep. Most have been lying
outdoors on the stony ground to catch the cool sea breeze, but quickly head inside as the
morning comes, for the respite that the shade of the orange plastic sheeting lends them. A few of
the young men rouse themselves and head off in search of a daily wage, but most just stay still.
Resting under their plastic bags of meagre possessions, tied above to the stick structure, for many
of the tahrib here lethargy sets in quickly, as they doze away their last days in Africa.
Located among a mass of tents at a coastal bush camp, the Oromo Hotel is just one of three such
doss houses run by the same smuggling gang.

Left

Having spent the last week waiting to hear news about the boat he hopes to take to Yemen, Said wakes up late in the morning in a daze, having spent the night sleeping on a straw mat at the Oromo Hotel.

Centre

Emerging from a back room, a tahrib throws his hands up in joy after counting out his money. He has nearly a million shillings, and will go to Yemen any day now.

Right

One of the tahrib's most common and treasured possessions are the miniature address books that they carry; usually waterproofed and protected by tying them tightly up in a plastic bag. They contain all of their contacts, and most importantly, details of smugglers and of friends in Yemen that they are hoping to look up. Storing numbers in a mobile phone is less secure, since these are frequently robbed by either smugglers or by the bandits that work Somalia's roads. With nothing to do, tahrib such as Chala can spend hours looking through their address books and often borrow telephones to put in missed calls to the people they hope to meet up with ahead of them on their journey.

"I fled Ethiopia because the police were harassing me. My father was a militant in the Ogaden Liberation Front and I am a student but the authorities accused me of being an OLF militant too. I fled with my seventeen year old sister Kenza who was threatened as well, and we travelled to Bossaso because we heard many Ethiopian people come here. Now we live at the Oromo Hotel; it's a shanty hut made of cardboard with only one room, where other migrants and refugees eat and sleep. At night, men and women rest directly on the floor. To survive, I've been working as a porter. I make only ten thousand shillings a day, which is just enough to pay for three meals and a night in the hotel. I can't find work every day so sometimes I cannot eat and I'm hungry. My sister works as a maid in a Somali house and she gives me money sometimes. Both of us make just enough to survive but nothing else. I am worried to cross to Yemen because it is very dangerous and because I fear that once there, the authorities might deport me back to Ethiopia where I'm in great danger."

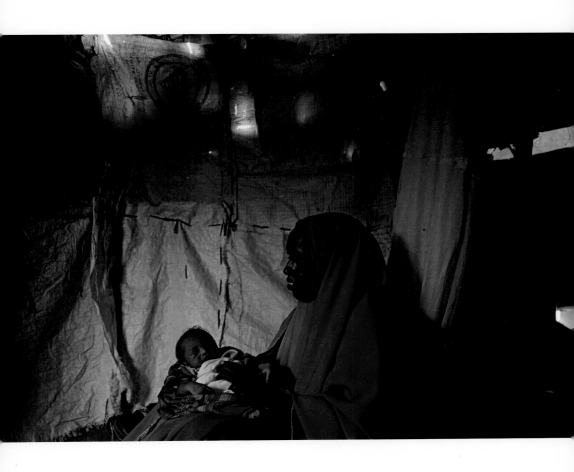

Living in a bush shelter constructed only of sticks, cardboard and wheat sacks pieced together with string, twenty two year old mother of three Hoda rests with her newborn baby girl Hazra, in an overcrowded camp on Puntland's coast.

Arriving in this supposed transit haven from Mogadishu with her husband a year ago, the couple planned to head across the Gulf of Aden with smugglers in search of a new life in Saudi Arabia. With only one place available on the boat, Hoda's husband went ahead. That was seven months ago. Presumed drowned, she has not heard word of him since.

Now Hoda is desperate to follow in his footsteps, along with her baby, in search of him. She cannot believe that he could have died, and wants only to see him again. "I can neither go back to Mogadishu with my children, as it is too dangerous there, nor stay in Bossaso, where there is only poverty for us. I am desperate to cross to Yemen. My ten-year old daughter is used to helping me with the youngest children, she will take care of them while I'm away. We cannot go on living in a squalid settlement for displaced people ... This is not a life."

Previous pages
Confined to a small dark shelter at the back of a halfway house in one of Bossaso's coastal camps, Fatima rests with her three day old baby son. Despite the risks that came with being heavily pregnant, Fatima and her husband decided to set out in search of a better life in Yemen rather than stay on and raise their child amid the bloodshed they witnessed in Mogadishu. For now, Fatima's husband is picking up sporadic casual work as a labourer in the port, as they save up the money to pay smugglers for their onward sea crossing. It could take him months to earn enough.

A displaced girl helps to cook a meal for a group of young tahrib in a shelter built from sticks on one of Bossaso town's windswept beaches. This flimsy doss house is run by a notorious, plump, qat-chewing mama. Renowned as Somalia's only female smuggler, she wins over new arrivals with her hospitality, but plays a level game with the men when it comes to coordinating the movement of the tahrib she collects. With thirty-five migrants and refugees currently hiding out in the shelter, it will take her another week to boost numbers, before she escorts them along with her militia to a remote stretch of coast, from where they will continue on their dangerous voyage to Yemen.

Juju charms of twigs and chains sit on a table in Bantu elder Mohamed Ali Juba's self-constructed family home built of branches and plastic sheeting. Marginalised in Somalia for being ethnically and culturally different, the Bantu tribe has been particularly vulnerable to abuses by militias throughout Somalia's clan warfare. Traditionally farmers, the Bantu have been on the run since the outbreak of civil war, and can be found in camps across Somalia and Yemen.

Following pages
Having just arrived after weeks on the road from Mogadishu, twenty year old
Kadra Abdi Shide rests on a mattress with her two severely malnourished
children, Nasethah and Howha, as they recover in a Phase II ward of the
MSF stabilisation centre. Coming to Bossaso with a group of five other
young women, Kadra and her children were identified by outreach workers
sheltering in the town's overrun Mingis Camp.

With the displaced in Bossaso's camps suffering such extreme hardships, they are prone to malnutrition and extremely vulnerable to both disease and death. With so many exhausted women and children arriving in the town after days spent on the road, the stabilisation centre for malnourished children at Biyo Kulule was set up by NGO Médecins Sans Frontières (MSF), in response early in 1997. Ambulatory teams located tens of underfed and dehydrated children on their daily visits to the surrounding settlements; the majority in dire circumstances. As fighting in Mogadishu escalated that spring, the numbers only got higher. The blue painted rooms of the hospital were filled with women cradling young babies, brushing off flies while their children lay almost lifeless as they underwent therapeutic feeding. Many were hoping that they would just get better quickly so that they could continue their journey out of Somalia. Others were just in a state of despair. A few months later the programme had to close after a doctor and nurse were kidnapped by one of the smuggling gangs. In the seven months the Biyo Kulule centre was open, two thousand children were admitted.

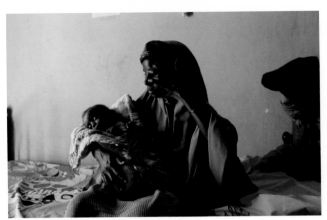

Previous pages and above
For this group of Somali and Ethiopian tahrib, the days of waiting nervously for their passage are long. There is little to do in the back alleys of Bossaso, and the smugglers are keen that their human cargo don't stray too far. In the heat of the afternoon, the group sits around smoking water pipes and sharing bags of the narcotic qat, that they chew and wash down with 7-Up and green tea. Most keep close their plastic bag of possessions - a spare T-shirt, a mobile phone, a shawl and maybe a radio and some cigarettes. They have brough little with them on their journey.
In less than two hours, station wagons will come and collect batches of ten passengers at a time. Transporting them to waiting trucks at the edge of one of the town's camps, armed gangs will then escort them to the Horn's remote beaches. Here they will spend their last nights at the tip of their home continent.

Expectant mother Fehir has spent nearly a month sleeping on the floor of a straw-covered hut in the courtyard of Elias's house. She has just less than a million shillings, and badly wants to take a boat to Yemen before the baby is born. It is due any day now and if she delivers she will have to pay more.

Pregnant and tired, Fatima sits next to people smuggler Elias. She has been helping to make tea and cook lately as she tries to make a few shillings. "In our village, my husband talked with some people who had been deported from Saudi Arabia. They were richer than us and lived in better houses. They told us that there were plenty of jobs in Saudi Arabia and that we should try our luck too. I travelled with my husband as we were supposed to go together to Yemen, but once we reached Bossaso, he told me he couldn't afford the crossing for the two of us and he went alone, abandoning me. That's when I found out I was pregnant. Now I feel sick, and I can't find work because people won't hire a woman in my condition who is not healthy. I spend my days in Ethiopian cafés hoping to receive help. I don't want to cross to Yemen anymore, I just want to go home but I have no money to pay for the return trip. Now I don't know what to do."

Testament to the hundreds of tahrib that have passed through this clandestine smuggler's house before, an Ethiopian refugee chewing a siwak stick looks after an unaccompanied minor in front of a backdrop of scrawled Amharic graffiti.

Above
A crudely constructed wooden box in the corner of "the office" houses an old television. Powered by a car battery, the box is also the only place where mobile phones can be charged, and with just a couple of power points it can be a scramble to get to.
Illuminated as pop videos play on the screen, smuggler Elias uses his phone to make contact with a truck driver as he coordinates the collection of some of his resident charges.

This is how it works here … Elias sends out his boys to pick up new arrivals as they come into town. Tired and disorientated, they are offered a place to sleep and often their first meal of spaghetti or rice on the house. Until they can pay Elias a million shillings, workers in the house make a little money selling cooked food and tea to the tahrib as they spend days or weeks waiting for their chance to go to sea. Once a group of around thirty or forty have paid-up, the boat owners are then informed and the onward journey is arranged. The majority of the money is paid to the heads of the smuggling gangs, but of course Elias takes his cut. He took over the abandoned fisherman's café two or three years ago, and he's doing good business.

A worker helps to turn out molds of fibreglass hulls at the Hiddig boatbuilding factory, located in the old industrial port area of Soweto on Bossaso's outskirts. With Somalia's traditional dhow building industry long in decline, fishermen and smugglers have had to look to the Arabian Peninsula to buy new lighter, faster fibreglass vessels. Now with the stolen molds, the Hiddig factory can produce the same small fishing boats for just a third of the price. Since the yard opened, affordable output means that more and more people are investing in a boat and joining the smuggling racket, and now even Yemenis are starting to come and buy on this side of the gulf. The owners of course have no interest in what the boats they turn out are used for, but they know that their best business comes from the pirates and human traffickers who fuel the economy across this lawless peninsula.

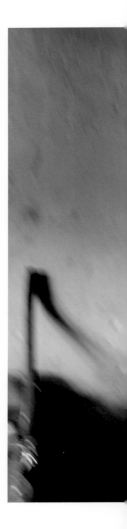

Visiting his lock-up in downtown Bossaso, smuggler Omar picks up a
bundle of a million shillings from his store of money, earned by ferrying
thousands of tahrib across the Gulf of Aden to Yemen each year. Equivalent
to just $50, this handful of cash is what each migrant or refugee pays to put
their destiny in the hands of such smugglers. It is the price of life here.

Following pages

Watching over a group of refugees at one of his network's safe houses hidden deep in Bossaso town's back streets, thirty-four year old "big fish" smuggler Omar lights a cigarette.

Working at sea since he was a teenager, Omar spent years helping local fishermen to hunt down sharks for their fins but illegal commercial fishing put an end to the business. He involved himself instead in the arms trade, ferrying weapons to and from Yemen. War in Somalia provided him with new financial rewards however when Bossaso became the country's hub in human trafficking as more and more people began to flee the brutal fighting while warlords tore the country apart. The profits for him are the main draw. He now makes a minimum of $5000 per month ferrying migrants and refugees across the Gulf of Aden to Yemen; far in excess of the average income of just $100 a month in Somalia.

Continued from page 91

Omar may be a "big fish" in Bossaso, but he is just part of a bigger countrywide chain. His unnamed network has offices in Mogadishu, Belet Weyne and Galkayo in southern Somalia, and Burao on the Ethiopian border. "These *tahrib* pay $20 to one of our offices before making their own way here - a receipt then guides them to me when they get here and I charge $50 to get them to Yemen, but then the boat owners and agents take commission, and of course we have to pay off the authorities". Omar is just one of eight key smugglers working in Bossaso linked to international networks of agents and traffickers. He shrugs off the violence and death perpetrated at the hands of his men. When he looks at the forty migrants in his charge waiting to board boats to Yemen that night, he calls them "blood money".

Having spent the last five days at sea and nearly three weeks travelling on the road, twenty six year old Ahmed Murr recovers along with fellow survivors, in the confines of smuggler Omar's safe house in Bossaso town.

Having survived being shot in the forehead during heavy fighting in Somalia's capital, Ahmed escaped the city with a group of friends. Coming from Mogadishu, they had few fears about the journey that lay ahead of them.

He thinks his friends are now in Yemen, having crossed the Gulf of Aden in the boats of Omar's men but he's not sure they are still alive. Ahmed was with them but he never made it ashore. Approaching a beach on Yemen's south-eastern coast in the dead of night, the tiny fishing boat in which they were travelling came under attack, as Yemeni soldiers fired randomly into the dark sea. He was one of the few survivors. Despite the captain being shot, the two remaining crew managed to turn the boat around and navigate their way back across the seas. Sailing with the captain's body and the five tahrib who had remained on board, it took them three more days to make it back to Bossaso. In total, they spent six days at sea without food or drinking water. Ahmed Murr is now ready to try again. He hopes to spend a few days resting, and has asked Omar to help him cross for a second time. There is no going back.

The Fourth Quarter

At the foot of Djiboutiville's African sector, where the road from Somalia terminates, a ghetto known since French colonial times as the *Quartier Quatre*, has become host to an influx of tahrib looking for another way across to Yemen. The slums surrounding this transit hub are now interpreted colloquially by residents as *Karte Katra*, or the Fourth Quarter.

As increasing numbers of refugees and migrants lose friends or relatives in their escape from Somalia, and the reputation of Bossaso's violent gangs becomes more notorious, a new route from Djibouti has opened up. Located just thirty kilometres across the busy shipping lanes of the Bab El-Mandeb Strait, the crossing to Yemen from here seems more appealing to those wishing to flee unrest in Africa's Horn. Despite the chances of dying being substantially lower due to the much shorter voyage, there are inherent gambles in attempting to traverse one of the continent's smallest and most heavily militarised countries.

For the tahrib en route to Djibouti from south central Somalia, the land journey is far longer and less straightforward than the one to Bossaso. Forced to pass through the autonomous state of Somaliland, they become conspicuous both when crossing the frontiers, and inside a territory that is comprised of ethnically different clans. As obvious outsiders, and without the benefit of the unwritten rules of tribal protection, refugees and migrants are more prone to extortion and frequently find themselves detained by the authorities. At worst, they can be imprisoned for months before being forced to turn back to the areas of violent conflict from which they have fled.

Even if the tahrib are able to navigate their way through Somaliland without incident, there is still the Djiboutian border to be negotiated. Most turn to guides, paying around thirty dollars each to lead them on the overnight journey on foot that takes them through rough terrain over arid mountains. Walking in small groups, routes are frequently altered as the authorities become wise to the increasing numbers of illegal immigrants, and the going can be especially hard for the frail and for women with young children.

As more than one thousand tahrib cross into Djibouti each week, in response to the new routes, a reception centre close to the Loyada frontier has been opened by UNHCR to help vulnerable refugees and those seeking asylum. For the refugees who are registered, trucks take arrivals on to the far-flung camp located out in the bleak desert at Ali-Addeh. The camp is home to more than seven thousand refugees housed in white tents that spread out across black volcanic stones. This arid place where it never rains offers nothing more than temporary security. Few settle for this life and most move quickly on.

Heading north to Djibouti's eponymous capital, trucks and minivans drop migrants and refugees in the bustling, dirty streets that surround the Fourth Quarter. Wide avenues that once carried trade from the port lead off to narrow, sewage filled lanes, where iron shacks fill every available space. In a part of town that, since colonial times, has been apportioned only for Africans, the squats in the Fourth Quarter that were previously home to generations of workers are now overcrowded warrens, where the competition for space has forced up rents in what is inexplicably Africa's most expensive country. New arrivals have few options when they come to look for shelter. The clandestine doss houses, run by smugglers that tout their business from telephone kiosks and restaurants around the bus stops, overcharge despite offering little more than tiny, shared spaces where occupants must take turns to lie down. As more and more tahrib stream into Djiboutiville, even single women and unaccompanied minors are forced to sleep out in the streets. Finding space between market stalls or on shop verandas, they expose themselves to the very real risk of robbery or abuse.

Unable to afford to hang around, and trapped amid the slums in a strange country, most of the tahrib are keen to move quickly. The logistics of the long journey however often detain them for longer periods than intended. As criminals move in on the smuggling racket, many simply disappear along with the money they have taken from the impoverished migrants and refugees, while other agents are regularly caught out as the authorities clamp down on gangs before they even attempt to move their human cargo out of town. Unlike Somalia where the smugglers work with impunity in what is lawless terrain, operations in Djibouti are frequently suspended as police roadblocks on the routes to remote beaches, catch those running the gauntlet to Yemen.

Those that find themselves on the streets of the Fourth Quarter have already on average spent two to three hundred dollars just to reach that far. It will cost them a further twenty thousand Djiboutian Francs - upwards of a hundred dollars - for the onward passage to Yemen. Uncertain about what their fate holds, or deceived and penniless, many discuss alternative ways out of this dead end part of town. They talk of going overland, through Eritrea, Sudan and Libya, picking up work as they go. Their new dreams are of Europe.

For those who do manage to pay funds to the more reputable gangs, the next stage in their journey from the Fourth Quarter will be on to the northerly beaches around the small fishing town of Obock. Located across the sweeping bay of Tadjura, the small backwater port with its crumbling factories and coral stone houses still bears scars from the country's recent civil war. A quiet outpost, it has long been notorious for the smuggling of cigarettes, alcohol and other contraband. From here only dusty tracks lead off to coastal fishing settlements, or run through the barren landscape that stretches north to the Eritrean border.

Most of the tahrib spend just a day or two in Obock and see little of the town. Arriving in the early hours of the morning, they are quickly hidden away in small fishermen's shacks or back alley squats, distinguished only by the debris and stench left behind by those who have passed through before. Concealed in dark rooms, local runners bring food, water and qat as the smuggling business becomes increasingly covert. Recent raids by the authorities have filled the town's tiny old French gaol with hundreds of migrants and refugees; their fate undecided.

From Obock's hideaways, it is a short night-time ride away to the beaches where the dhow operators collect their human cargo for the short sea voyage to Yemen's western shores. The risks now are of being caught in the lights of patrolling navies, and the dangerous crossing in which the small wooden boats navigate their way between huge container vessels at the mouth of the Red Sea.

With a television set playing films or local pop videos late into the night, the street cafes in Djibouti's African quarter provide a place to congregate for those in transit. For the price of a cup of tea, they can while away the hours. Chit-chat amongst the refugees revolves around where they can sleep, the latest smugglers' offices to have opened in town, and contacts for the road ahead.

Covering their bodies with tattered blankets and veils, a group of thirty female refugees spend the
night sleeping along the pavement in Djiboutiville's Rue Issa. Having fled the escalating fighting in
Mogadishu, this group of women arrived in Djibouti just three days before.
Record numbers crossing the porous border has lead to serious overcrowding in the city's slums.
For these already vulnerable women, there are no shelters, no place of refuge at the mosques and
nowhere left to turn to, as the already impoverished city dwellers start to charge exorbitant rents,
that remain unaffordable to all but a few of the tahrib. Testament to this, females have now been
seen sleeping out in the open for the first time. Most have paid what little money they have to
bed their children down for the night in a place of safety; they don't have enough shillings spare
to put themselves out of harm's way.

Following pages
Just before the 9pm curfew, Somali refugees head to the Makfir Mosque in Djiboutiville's Fourth Quarter in the hope of finding somewhere safe to spend the night. As thousands of migrants and refugees fleeing violence in south central Somalia arrive in Djibouti each week, overcrowding in the small capital forces many to sleep on the dirty streets, putting themselves at risk of attack or robbery. Three of the city's mosques are now opening their doors to those in need, including the Makfir, which currently provides space for seventy refugees in its main prayer hall, many of whom are lone young boys. After nine o'clock however, the Imam has no choice but to turn many away - there is just no space.

Disembarking in the evening from a truck that has brought them from the Somaliland border, best friends Faisal Abdulahi Tahlil and Ahmed Hassan Hersi hold hands as they set off anxiously through streets of Djibouti, looking for somewhere to sleep. Carrying with them only a light jacket, a shirt and a comb in a small backpack, the two young men have spent the last six weeks on the road from Mogadishu, paying their way bit by bit by picking up badly paid jobs, including a week spent breaking rocks in Galkayo. Hungry and tired, their first stop is at a restaurant where they hope to look for a contact they have heard might be of help. Unable to find him, they instead bed down with a group of other tahrib in the streets of the city's Fourth Quarter.

Short of funds for the boat journey with smugglers to Yemen, Faisal and Ahmed have instead decided to try their luck by heading overland to Eritrea. They hope that by continuing in the same vein as on the road from Mogadishu, they can pick up work en-route and continue through the deserts to Sudan and Libya. Their dream destinations are Italy or the UK, where each has relatives. Having grown up knowing nothing but war, they are undeterred by the dangers that may lie ahead, "If we stay in Somalia any longer, death will come to us".

Visiting a cafe located opposite the Somaliland bus terminal that is popular with newly arrived tahrib, Faisal and Ahmed enquire about a place to sleep, having spent their first night in Djibouti on the streets.

Having lost all his possessions to thieves on the road from Mogadishu, Abdul Majid feels lucky to have hung onto his favourite camouflage baseball cap and England T-shirt; his shoes are long gone. Like many teenagers fleeing Somalia's capital, his parents have encouraged him to leave, fearing that like other young men, he will be captured by the Shabaab militia, and either killed or forced to fight in their ranks. Abdul says he is eighteen years old, but looks younger.

Since arriving in Djibouti with the aid of smugglers at Somaliland's mountainous border fifteen days ago, he has been sleeping on the street beside a mosque, and begging around the cafes of the Fourth Quarter for free meals. Despite having got word to his family that he has now arrived in Djibouti, he is still waiting for them to forward money so that he can continue to Yemen - it could still take some time but they have promised it will come soon. Two years ago they paid for Abdul's older brother Mohamed Daeq's boat fare from Bossaso. He was killed by smugglers on the crossing, but upon hearing that new safer routes have since opened up, they are taking the opportunity to give their other son a chance in life.

Although particularly vulnerable as an unaccompanied minor, Abdul has plenty of enthusiasm for the journey, and has heard that if at any stage he is captured by the authorities, then his youth will protect him. Among the other tahrib in the city's Fourth Quarter though, he looks small and nervous, belying his confident exterior. Biting his nails he boasts, "When I reach to Sana'a or Saudia, then I will have enough money for me and my family".

Hearing a tip-off at a café that morning, Abdul Majid accompanies two other newly arrived
tahrib to the shanty house of a female Somali refugee, who is rumoured to be helping young boys
with nowhere to stay. As she watches television with her children in a dirty blue room, Abdul is
discouraged. She says that without work she can't afford the exorbitant rent on the one-roomed
shack and is looking for some temporary lodgers so as to abate the threats from her landlord.
For Abdul it's a dead end. He will spend the rest of the day searching around the narrow back
streets but competition for a place to sleep seems tough.

Following pages
Nine year old Kali Abduhi Omar stares at her reflection in the screen of a broken television set,
as she sits in a make-shift room in one of Djiboutiville's illicit doss houses.
Following a mortar strike on her family's home in central Mogadishu, Kali and her younger
brother have just arrived in Djibouti after spending weeks on the road. Their exhausted mother
curled up in the corner of the room is sick, and scarred from bullet wounds she sustained in the
attack. Four other Somali women and their children share the cramped space with Kali, as they
wait to hear news from a female contact about the smugglers who could help them continue on
their journey to Yemen.

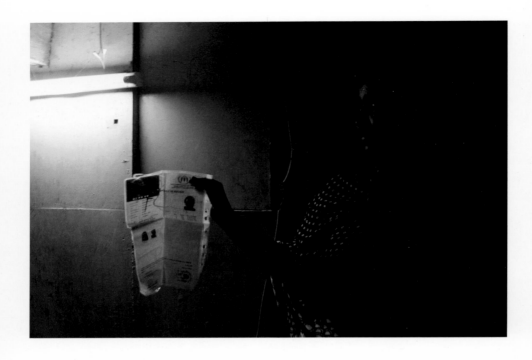

Under the dim glow of a strip light, Kali's mother Farhiya Kasim Abdulle holds up the refugee identity paper issued to her and her family by UNHCR upon arrival at Djibouti's Ali Addeh Camp. After losing her husband in a mortar strike that hit their home, injured Farhiya grabbed her two children and fled the Huriwaa neighbourhood of Mogadishu, otherwise known as "Fallujah". Barely able to walk and covered in shrapnel wounds, she is looking for a way to find sanctuary in Yemen. After twelve days spent on the road, for now she just needs to rest.

Where the African and European quarters meet, a street lined with telephone
booths and money changing offices, run by refugees who have made their
base here, provide services for the newly arrived tahrib of Djibouti.
Behind a curtained door on a small intersection sits an inconsequential grocery
store selling drinks, chewing gum, and sweets. A young boy mans the counter
as the female owner Fylis chats to the men taking sodas outside. Behind the
shelves, a flimsy partition hides a clandestine halfway house known as the
"Hamawiri Shop", after the local slang for people from Mogadishu.
Around thirty tahrib on average stay here at a time. The ramshackle
construction seems to barely hold up the weight of this tiny terraced house.
Only two buzzing fluorescent bulbs cast any light in this windowless interior.
A ladder built of wooden planks nailed together at angles leads up to a
precarious landing where the thin floor can only be navigated by tiptoeing
on the rafters. Four tiny rooms partitioned with plywood and plastic sheeting
tightly house the temporary residents, in conditions that are unbearably hot
and stuffy. The Hamawiri Shop is grim, but for the refugees there it's only a
stop gap, and a world away from Mogadishu.

Staying with his widowed mother at the Hamawiri Shop for the past two weeks, eight year old Mohamed Abdullah Omar sits at the top of a ladder outside the room that his family share with three female refugees and their children.

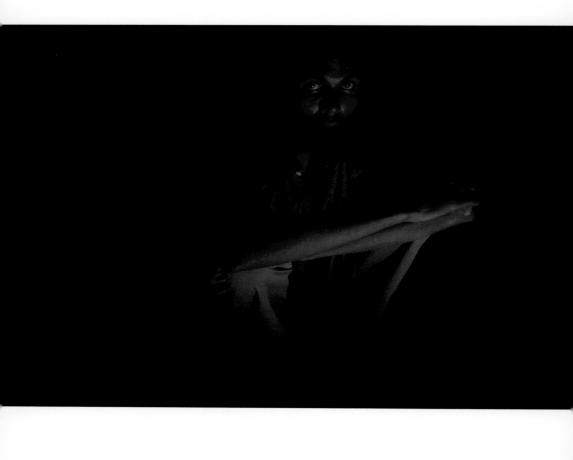

Up on the roof, planks of wood prop up little corrugated iron shelters overlooking the street below. Filled with plastic bags and luggage, these are the rooms in which the young men resident at the Hamawiri Shop spend their nights, side by side on flattened cardboard boxes. The rooms downstairs are reserved for the women and children who require more privacy.

Following pages

Fast asleep on a bed of cardboard, twenty eight year old Abas Hassan Ulusow spends the night out in the open, on the rooftop of the Hanwari Shop in the centre of Djiboutiville. After fighting in Mogadishu devastated his home, Abas fled Somalia with the dream of making it to Yemen and being able to support his family. Still holding out for funds from relatives with which to pay the smuggling gangs for the onward sea crossing, a week after he arrived here Abas is anxious to proceed with his journey but worried about the high prices being charged. Rumours are rife in town that the smugglers' middlemen are taking fares from the tahrib and then quickly disappearing. After chatting with new-found friends, he is now contemplating setting off to follow the dangerous overland route through Eritrea, Sudan and Libya, that could eventually bring him to Europe.

Sharing a thin foam mattress with three other friends from Mogadishu, all planning to travel to Yemen, Abdi Mohamed Abdullah sleeps under a corrugated iron shelter on the Hamawiri Shop's rooftop.

Fleeing Mogadishu last year after being wounded in the neck by shrapnel during heavy fighting, nineteen year old Ahmed Ibrahim is now on his second bid to reach Yemen. Having travelled with smugglers on a boat from Bossaso nine months ago, Ahmed was lucky to make it across the Gulf of Aden alive. He saw fellow passengers being beaten by an enraged crew that threw one young boy overboard just for complaining. Capsizing close to a landing site on the Arabian Peninsula, Ahmed was just one of a few survivors. Barely able to swim, he can only thank Allah for saving his life. Eventually arriving in Sana'a, Ahmed spent four months washing cars but disillusioned with the life he found in Yemen, headed to Saudi Arabia with the little money he saved. Despite finding work tending cattle, he was quickly caught by the police, imprisoned due to his illegal status and deported back to Mogadishu. With his dreams shattered, no home or family left to return to and the security situation deteriorating, his only thought was to try and escape for a second time. He is too scared to see the smugglers in Bossaso to whom he entrusted his life with before, and on hearing of new routes from Djibouti while in prison, is trying his luck from here with a gang of boat-owning Afars. For now, Fylis has given him a place to sleep at the Hamawiri Shop that is out of sight. He prays that he will reach Obock any day now, and things will work out better for him the second time round.

Saara Ali Mohamed comforts her friend Ayan Mousa Esmail in an overcrowded room of a transit house. The two eighteen year old girls both escaped from Mogadishu after their homes were destroyed in an attack by Ethiopian forces during the recent wave of fighting. Hiding out along with twenty-two other tahrib, both are waiting to travel with smugglers across the Gulf of Aden to Yemen. Having met on the road in an overland journey that took them three weeks, this new group of friends now refer to themselves as "the gang", and are hoping to continue the onward leg of their journey together. They know that it will be the most dangerous part but have consciously come via Djibouti in order to avoid the notorious smugglers in Bossaso that they have heard so much about. So far they have only made contact with middle men in Djibouti, via the owners of a small money exchange office, and know little about the reputations of the local smugglers in whose hands they will ultimately place their lives.

Noor Jimale looks at his reflection in one of the girl's pocket mirrors, as he rests on the floor of the overcrowded room that "the gang" are sharing. There is barely enough room inside the flimsy shack to stretch out at night, and so most of the temporary male and female residents take turns to nap or lie down during the hot day.

Lying in a row under sheets, childhood friends Ahmed Moalin, Mohamed Mousa and Sharmake Abdulahi, thumb through their fake passports. Purchased for $50 each on the streets of Mogadishu, con men have simply filled in the stolen documents with the details of the boys, making their entries into Somaliland and Djibouti an easy affair. Coming from a country where few people have ever set eyes on official paperwork, the forged passports have become objects of fascination within the gang of tahrib. They won't need them to travel to Yemen on smugglers' boats but are hanging on to them just in case things go wrong. There has been plenty of talk about overland routes to Europe, and they think they could prove useful in the long run.

Often just a shack showing old action films or Bollywood movies on video,
so-called cinemas dot the streets and bazaars of Djiboutiville's African
Quarter. For just a few francs or shillings, it is possible to find a place to sit
for an entire day out of the sun, with a little entertainment thrown in. Usually
furnished with rows of wooden benches, the cinemas attract passing refugees
looking for a distraction; many even use the venues as a place to lay their
heads for a few hours. Exhausted, they sleep soundly as the rattle of gunfire
for once, bursts from the television screen.

Sheltering in a tent that she shares with three other families, twenty-six year old Nimo Abdi sits with her three year old son Sadiiq. After her husband and two other children were killed in an explosion in Mogadishu, Nimo fled to her sister's house, only to be told that she had left for Djibouti. In search of her remaining family, Nimo set out on the long journey to track her down. A year later and she is stuck in the remote Ali Addeh Camp trying to care for Sadiiq, who is suffering from severe mental disturbances; she thinks a result of the almost continuous shelling he endured as a baby in Somalia. Nimo feels trapped here, and never imagined her life would turn out like this. She has never found her sister.

At a tent in the far-flung Ali Addeh Camp refugees make signs protesting at their plight. Located in a remote inland desert near the Somaliland border, the camp is often just a pit stop on the journey for the tahrib but home to more than seven thousand long-term Somali and Ethiopian refugees.

As authorities round up those crossing illegally into Djibouti at its southern border, trucks ferry groups of refugees from the Loyada frontier to Ali Addeh, where they are registered by UNHCR and offered shelter. Conditions here are bleak, with residents surviving hand to mouth on food and water distributions. The solitude of the place and the harsh environment mean that only the very vulnerable and those seeking asylum or formal relocation to a third country stay put. With new smuggling routes across the Bab El-Mendab Strait opening up, the numbers passing through the camp have dramatically increased. During the first month that smugglers began operations in Dijbouti, the same number of refugees were registered as were expected for the whole year.

For those who have made Ali Addeh home, there is a strong feeling that they have been marginalised; pushed out into this barren land by the Djiboutian authorities so they can be forgotten.

As the group of refugees hold up their banners, a teenage girl called Farah sits crying in the corner. "I lost my mum and dad in Mogadishu, I came home and my house was burning. I'm a refugee now but I never wanted to end up like this. I've been here for a month now and I don't know how the others have resisted. I would prefer to die in the sea".

At the northern tip of the Gulf of Tadjoura, sleepy fishing ports such as Obock have long had a reputation as smugglers' havens. Alcohol, cigarettes and illicit contraband are frequently ferried across the short stretch of water to Yemen from here. Lately however the dhows have been transporting a rather more profitable cargo.

In this hot and dusty one street town, small groups of tahrib are carefully hidden away, often forbidden from walking out during the day. Runners bring supplies of soft drinks, cigarettes and qat back to the fly-infested wooden shacks, where the disorientated refugees rarely spend more than a day or two. Heading north along the coast to distant beaches, Yemen is just four hours away across the narrow Bab El-Mendab Strait. To have made it this far means that escape is achingly close.

Goodbye Somalia

None of the tahrib in Bossaso really know what will happen; only that they need to be ready when the time comes. After restless days and weeks spent thinking of loved ones left behind and dreaming of the uncertain life that may lie ahead, the order to proceed can come suddenly without warning. The smuggling gangs are well-practiced at coordinating high numbers and like to move swiftly. The departure from Somalia will come quickly now for the migrants and refugees.

The tahrib never move too far from the few belongings they have brought. They learn to conceal the items that are precious to them for fear of robbery or being drenched out at sea. Saved or spare shillings are changed into single dollar bills, and like the tiny address books and mementos from home, they are wrapped tightly in pieces of plastic which are then tied around the top of their arms or legs beneath a sleeve or a sarong. Advised by the middlemen who have acted as their guardians, most have packed some biscuits, dried dates or cans of tuna to sustain them on the voyage. These things can be grabbed in a second.

From the outset, everything is done in tens. When a smuggler has collected together all his fares and enough tahrib to fill a boat with no space to spare, only then can the passengers be picked up from their halfway houses. Fingers will be pointed, and those chosen are summoned. They are bundled into hatchback cars with tinted windows, fur trimmed dashboards and Islamic-themed air fresheners, before being taken to the town's outer limits. On the edge of tattered camps, there is only desert ahead of them. Until the hatchbacks have shuttled back and forth around a dozen times, they must wait under an awning where the boat captains play cards. The migrants and refugees sit hunched up in silence.

As numbers build and the gang leaders show up with their truck driver friends, the atmosphere becomes agitated. Congregating in an open space, and operating seemingly unnoticed by those around them, the men and women are piled into flatbed lorries. The smugglers begin to flail their arms barking commands, while crying babies onboard the trucks are comforted by mothers. This is the last point in the journey that they can turn back, and so the tahrib climb on board hesitantly. With armed guards around them, it already seems too late; there is no return.

The trucks proceed along a featureless shoreline patrolled only by militia and hyenas. After thirty kilometres, the dry red desert plains give way to mountains that sweep steeply down into a series of broad sandy bays. Arriving after nightfall, the tahrib are dropped off between dark rocks. The beaches where they will spend their last night in Somalia are eerie, frightening spaces. Feeling their way, the migrants and refugees search for places of shelter out of the strong winds that whip in from the shore. The good spots are filled with debris and faeces, evidence of the tens of thousands that have passed through here before them. There is a feeling of total isolation but with numbers scattered throughout the caves and cliffs, distant sounds of low voices and coughing signal that they are far from alone.

Stoked on qat, the militia and boat crews camped out between barrels of fuel stay up until the early hours, joking around and playing with rifles. This is when the rapes and robberies frequently occur. Many of the Somalis have consciously separated themselves from the Ethiopians, who as foreigners are generally subjected to harsher treatment. Sleep does not come easily. Keeping still and out of sight, the migrants and refugees breath heavily in time to the incessant sound of the breaking waves.

After the long, sleepless night, most of the bodies remain motionless. Keeping their eyes closed, the tahrib try to rest a little better before the sun rises behind the mountains and the heat of the day kicks in. When the light becomes too fierce, they begin to rouse themselves. Hundreds of figures shrouded in sheets simultaneously take in a strange landscape, that they are seeing properly for the first time. Most are fixated on the boats moored just a few hundred metres away off-shore that will, "inshalla'ah" (God willing), soon be taking them across the gulf's horizon.

Much of what happens now depends on the mood of the smugglers and the crews. Supplies have to be brought in from Bossaso, and the likelihood is that the priority will be more cigarettes after a night spent chain-smoking. Usually, they insist on waiting until the afternoon qat flight lands in order to have fresh batches for the voyage. Still in town, the captains will make calls to their contacts in Yemen to check for reports from potential landing sites. If they feel cautious, they might also inquire about incoming storms; prevalent in the Gulf of Aden between May and August each year when summer monsoons sweep in. They have held off leaving for the beaches until the last minute, and it matters little to them to keep their human cargo waiting, even if it is for a couple of days.

As the refugees linger, they spend this anxious time sitting together under shaded rock overhangs or perched high up in the cliffs like birds. Some take short walks to the water's edge, looking out across the sea. By now, used to long drawn-out waits, the time on the beaches is even more restless and full of dread. Few have been on a boat before and know full well that the journey they are about to undertake could be their last. If they are lucky, they will leave the same day. Extra nights spent here will leave them tired and weak, their meagre rations for the voyage depleted.

When the captains eventually arrive then the "big fish" smugglers swing into action once again, coordinating a drill that has been practiced on this lawless edge of Africa's Horn for almost twenty years. Militia begin to wave their Kalashnikovs around, firing off rounds as they summon the refugees to the shore. With two or three boats often leaving together, the scene on the beach appears like a wayward military operation. The migrants and refugees with their plastic bags and jerry cans of drinking water are split into boatloads and made to crouch at gunpoint. Friends and family that have been separated try to reconvene but are threatened with rifle barrels. Those who do not obey orders or display misgivings risk being dragged away to face summary execution.

The captains and crew are the first to board their boats. Equipped with satellite phones, GPS navigation equipment and automatic weapons, they are able to call to their colleagues in case of trouble at sea and can easily deal with any disquiet. Once they have checked all is in order, they signal back to shore.

The migrants and refugees are separated, once again into groups of ten. Lined up they are pushed towards the sea by the militia who march them through the waves towards the anchored boats. Young children are carried aloft on shoulders, while women are helped by those wading behind them, their soaked dresses restricting their steps through the currents. In often deep water, it takes time for the crew to haul aboard the sodden refugees, and so the next group of ten are held back for a short while.

Inside what were former fishing boats, men are ordered down into the claustrophobic hull, to an enclosed compartment meant for storing ice to keep fish fresh. Exposed to the elements, the women are seated above, and ordered to place their knees tightly under their chin to save space. Instructed not to move, the one hundred and twenty or so refugees on board are then often tied together with rope to keep the boat more stable. Sitting curled up in their wet clothes the constricted passengers quickly get cold, as the three hundred kilometre plus journey gets underway.

For the next two to three days, the refugees must try to stay as still as possible no matter how uncomfortable they are; any movement will risk a beating. The toilet is the place where they are seated. Protests can be met with violent attacks or shootings, but more often the crew prefer to throw the noncompliant overboard into the Gulf of Aden's rough waters.

If the boat should capsize, the refugees have little chance of survival. Tied together or trapped inside, most would never even freely escape. Few are able to swim and there is almost no chance of rescue for them; they are left to the sharks.

On the now near empty beach, the smugglers watch their latest batch of human cargo disappear out into the open sea. Whatever the fate of the tahrib on board, each boatload has netted them $6,000. Tomorrow they will return to the beaches to begin again.

Right
Making their way on foot in high winds, part of a group of sixty Somali and Ethiopian tahrib head along the rubbish-strewn beach in Bossaso at sundown. Staying at a halfway house in one of the coastal camps, the men, women and children will convene for the first time after nightfall, and then meet with the smugglers and trucks that will eventually transport them to a remote departure point, from where they will say their goodbyes to Africa. Until the sun disappears, they hang around on the beach, reflecting on the long journey they have made so far and the more dangerous leg that lies just ahead.

Surrounded by burning rubbish, a former guesthouse that in its heyday catered to Italian sailors, sits on the dirty rock-covered shoreline close to the port in Bossaso.

Rough stone tracks mark the coastal routes out of Bossaso town. For the first few kilometres they lead down to dilapidated fish-processing plants, ice-making factories, leather works and boat yards that have long since closed following the decline of local industries. There is little reason to travel these roads and the journeys made on them are almost all clandestine. Checkpoints hidden behind boulders and in cliffs are manned by militia loyal to the smuggling gangs who control the length of this lawless shore. Only trucks packed full of tahrib on their way to departure points for Yemen, or the cars of the gang leaders, boat owners and organisers move here.

Around thirty kilometres out of town as the road becomes more difficult to negotiate, the flat plains give way to mountains that are reputed to hide Al-Qaeda training camps and weapons caches. Dropping down to sweeping sandy beaches on the turquoise Gulf of Aden, this is literally a smugglers' paradise.

Travelling in the back of a hatchback with smugglers, a young organiser heads to one of the doss houses near Bossaso port. Coordinating the collection of a group of tahrib who will be leaving Somalia that night, cars will shuttle ten at a time to a canvas shelter on the edge of town over the course of the afternoon. Not until a boatload of one hundred and twenty or so migrants and refugees are convened together, at what is the final rendezvous point, will the smugglers start to operate more freely. From this point on, they exercise complete control and can begin moving their human cargo onto trucks destined for Puntland's beaches without fear.

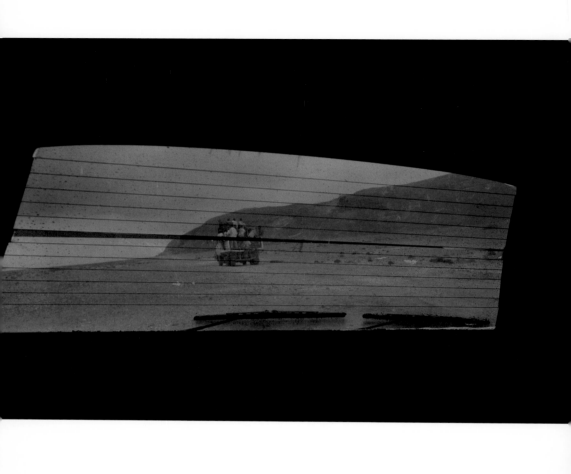

Overloaded with migrants and refugees, a truck makes its way along the rocky coastal road between Bossaso and the smugglers' cove of Marero.

Shuttling small groups of tahrib to an assembly point on the far edge of the town, a driver makes a pick-up from Elias' house - an old café that serves as a doss house for transiting Ethiopian migrants and refugees on their way to Yemen.

On their way to the beaches that serve as departure points for Yemen, flatbed trucks packed full of tahrib travel along coastal tracks. While some migrants and refugees are instructed to make the thirty kilometre journey along the shore on foot, most are openly shuttled in small batches by cheaply hired trucks. Escorted by armed gang members, the drivers can often make this journey several times a day in peak periods. With loyal militia in charge of the roads surrounding Bossaso, when it comes to these operations, there is little risk involved for the smugglers. For the tahrib, it is a short, uncomfortable ride, and just another stage in their long journeys.

Armed with Kalashnikovs, boat crew and militia from smuggler Abdullah's gang, make
preparations for the departure of a doon that will leave that night packed full of human cargo.
Sheltered behind rocks above Marero Beach, they stand amid the plastic bottles and debris
discarded by the some of the thousands of tahrib that transit through here each year. While the
migrants and refugees become anxious to depart, and a cold evening wind blows in, the crew
must first arrange for their supplies of cigarettes and qat to be brought from town.

Sheltered under a cliff overhang at Marero, migrants and refugees wait to leave Somalia on smugglers' boats that are being prepared for departure on the beach below. Unlike most of the tahrib who pay a million shillings for the crossing in over-packed and unstable vessels, the men in this group have paid three times the price to travel in smaller, faster boats that carry just thirty to forty people; most are economic migrants on their way to Saudi Arabia. Just along the cliffs, a group of women and children sit quietly on plastic sheeting. Leaving in the same boats, they are also headed to Saudi Arabia - but they are being trafficked. Promised jobs in the houses of rich families, their escape from Somalia is for free but they are likely to be sold and then enslaved for the rest of their lives. Hidden away from society and concealed behind their abayas, very few females are ever discovered by the authorities. Like thousands of other impoverished women from the Horn of Africa who are promised better lives in The Kingdom each year, they risk losing their freedom, rights and own name, becoming only "abid". The fate of the unaccompanied minors could be even worse. Unprotected and vulnerable, they are susceptible not only to slavery, but to sexual or physical abuse.

Lying against the rocks with his Kalashnikov, Abdu Rahman relaxes with a fellow armed gang member above the bay at Ras Marero beach. Originally from Mogadishu, Abdu is paid ten dollars a day by one of Bossaso's chief smugglers, to work as part of a security team, escorting migrants and refugees to the beaches. Notorious for their thuggish behaviour, the guards care little for the welfare of the thousands of tahrib that are put in their charge each year. High on hashish and qat, they are prone to firing their weapons in order to demonstrate their authority, or simply when they are fooling around. Known to rob, rape and even murder the vulnerable tahrib waiting to depart Somalia, Abdu and his friends show little mercy.

As the sun sets over the Gulf of Aden, a refugee waiting to depart from Ras Marero speaks to his family as he makes a final call from Somalia.

Waking up to their last dawn in Somalia, a tired group of tahrib rub their eyes as they take their first look at the landscape of Ras Shimbiro. Dropped off by smugglers' trucks in the early hours of the morning, they have spent a restless night laid out amid the rocks in total darkness. Few have slept properly. The incessant noise of a rip tide, along with the wailing of hyenas, the clicking of Kalashnikov clips, and the noise of cries and coughing from motionless bodies, have made this an uncomfortable night. As the smugglers and militia sleep soundly surrounded by barrels of petrol, the migrants and refugees sit still for now, too nervous to venture far. Most of the voyagers fix their eyes on three small boats anchored at the shore. It will be evening before they embark with the three hundred other passengers, and set off on the dangerous voyage across the Gulf of Aden to Yemen.

Having filled their jerry cans with fresh water from a nearby well, a group of sixty male migrants and refugees carrying tiny bundles of possessions wrapped in plastic bags, crouch tightly together on the pebbly shore at Marero. Receiving instructions from members of a smuggling gang, they have been told to line up in tens as they prepare to depart on boats that will take them on a two day voyage to Yemen. Sitting at some distance along the beach, women, children and the elderly will be boarded separately, and if lucky receive assistance, as they are marched into the water. Waiting as the crew load final supplies onto a boat moored some distance out in the shallow low tide, spots of rain fall from the heavy clouds. There is a storm brewing out at sea but the smugglers seem determined to leave before bad weather delays this shipment of human cargo. As volleys of gunfire ring out from the nearby cliffs, the tahrib are reminded that despite the risks ahead, there is no going back now.

Spending a second day hiding out in the mountains of Marero, eight year old Hassan and ten year old Mohamed rest on plastic sheeting as they wait to depart on the voyage across the Gulf of Aden. Having travelled from Mogadishu alone, the unaccompanied minors are now being escorted by an unrelated adult who will guide them to Saudi Arabia. Part of a boatload of Somalis who are being trafficked, the boys are nervous about the journey that lies ahead of them. Their guide has told them that he will help Hassan and Mohamed to find jobs and look after them; the likelihood however is that they will be sold upon reaching Saudi, only to be enslaved and abused.

Resting with his Kalashnikov in his lap, a member of a smuggling gang naps in the front seat of a car having spent the night standing guard over sleeping tahrib at Ras Shimbiro. Not anticipating that the waiting boats will depart for Yemen until evening, the militia and boat crews at the beach will spend the day relaxing as they watch over their next batch of human cargo.

Above and top right

Carrying plastic bags filled with biscuits, dried dates and some spare clothes for the journey, migrants and refugees make their way up into the steep cliffs above Shimbiro Beach as they prepare to spend a further night waiting to depart from Somalia. Groups gather and try to make themselves comfortable between the crags, while others perch nervously high above the water below. Translated from Somali, this headland on Africa's Horn is called "the place of birds". Bad weather and preparations by boat crews often delay departures from the beaches around Bossaso, forcing the tahrib to spend nights camped out amid the rocky cliffs. By the time they are boarded onto the small fishing boats that will take them on the two day voyage across the Gulf of Aden, most have finished off the meagre supplies brought with them. Already tired, weak and hungry, the most dangerous and grueling part of their journey still lies ahead.

After a whole night and day spent waiting to leave with smugglers from
Shimbiro Beach, a group of tired male tahrib hang around a small boat at
the shore's edge. Damaged by shelling as its crew came under fire by Yemeni
forces on the far side of the gulf, smugglers plan to repair the doon so that
it can be put back in action as soon as possible. While they mourn the
crewmembers killed, the gang will wait a week or so before approaching the
deceased captain's wife to ask for the vessel.

Women duck behind rocks as they run under a barrage of heavy gunfire in the mountains backing Shimbiro Beach. Waiting to depart on the smugglers' boats, the already terrorised passengers are put in further danger by the drunk and well-armed boat crew. Having already openly executed three tahrib on the beach, after they became too terrified to board a waiting doon, organisers are now insisting that others come back down from the cliffs. To the laughing smugglers, it is an exercise in control. The women eventually return to the beach sheepishly. As the firing continues they have little choice but to obey the demands.

As smugglers run back and forth through the water making last minute preparations, a crew member from a boat moored off the coast at Shimbiro returns to shore with a hammer. Many of the tiny fishing boats used by the smuggling networks are unreliable; as engines fail and the unstable vessels take on water, they frequently run into difficulties on the high seas. After carrying out repairs to the floating vessel, now packed with its human cargo, the hammer will subsequently be used as a weapon against the tahrib.

Ushered by boat crews and armed militia, an orderly column of male and female migrants and refugees carry jerry cans of fresh water and a few possessions wrapped in plastic bags, as they wade out into the sea from Shimbiro Beach. Heading to a smuggler's boat moored out in neck-deep water, these are their final steps on Somali soil.

Boat crew and so called organisers become aggressive, shouting and forcibly pushing waiting tahrib on the beach at Shimbiro. At the end of a long day's preparations, the atmosphere at the remote departure site becomes heated, as smugglers hurry their human cargo onto waiting boats before the sun sets.

Having spent the last twenty four hours camped out on Shimbiro's sandy beach, a group of young male migrants and refugees crowd onto a rock after a long tense day spent waiting to depart on smuggler's boats. Already tired having spent weeks on Somalia's roads just to get this far, their last few hours in Africa are filled with both longing and trepidation.

Previous pages and above

As smugglers make final preparations, migrants and refugees are lined up into rows, ready to board three waiting doons. Under a bright blue sky, the well-practiced military-style operation will see the passengers placed into groups of one hundred and twenty, before being ordered out to tiny former fishing boats in rows of ten. Armed militia stand guard in the background as the smugglers work quickly. The migrants and refugees who have been sitting in the sand for the past few hours must suddenly grab their belongings as they are marched quickly into the sea. In less than one hour, the beach will be almost empty again. The leaders of the smuggling gangs stay on shore, waiting for the crew to tie-up their human cargo before the boats slip anchor and are finally bound for Yemen. They can feel happy now. Each of the tahrib on board has paid a million Somali shillings for the journey; in total they have made $18,000 from this single operation.

Carrying a few meagre possessions, some dried food and a jerry can of water each for the journey, a line of ten male and female tahrib walk out into the blue waters of the Gulf of Aden. Heading for one of three waiting smuggling boats moored in neck-deep water, they will have to be hauled on board one by one by the crew. Coordinating such big numbers can be a headache for the smugglers but the crews prefer to make the journey in groups of two or three boats in case they encounter problems en-route. Carrying GPS navigation devices and satellite phones, should one of the vessels experience engine trouble or take on water, the crews can at least save themselves. For the one hundred plus migrants and refugees they leave out in the shark-infested high seas, it's another story.

Following pages
As a woman struggles to walk through the sea in high winds, a fellow passenger takes her by the hand as they head out to moored smugglers' boats near the coast at Ras Shimbiro.

Modified with sticks and plastic sheeting to help keep out water in the rough open seas, the boats have the same look as many of the shelters in which the migrants and refugees have camped on their long journeys this far. Some are painted with the logos of international NGOs, having been seized by the smugglers after boats equipped with new faster engines were donated to Somali fishermen, following the 1994 Indian Ocean tsunami. In such a remote, lawless area, the pirates and smugglers will take advantage of anything that helps sustain their criminal businesses at sea.

Previous pages

Standing in choppy shoulder deep water, Somali refugees look back anxiously from the sea as
they try to locate friends and relatives left behind on Shimbiro Beach. Preparing to board one of
three smugglers' boats that will depart simultaneously for Yemen, many of the passengers have
become separated from those that they had hoped to make this high-risk journey with.
As the crew haul passengers from the water, each is already soaking wet as they step onboard.
Before they even depart, the one hundred and twenty eight Somalis and Ethiopians tied down
inside the tiny boat begin to shiver as strong winds blow in from the sea. Their fate is now sealed.
Only eleven of the people who took this boat were ever to reach Yemen alive.

Above left

Preparing to depart at dusk, crew members roll barrels of petrol along the sandy beach ready to load onto waiting doons moored out in choppy waters. Supplies of fuel must be enough to cover the return journey from Yemen, and allow for a couple of days extra mileage should the boats have to evade capture, or make detours if they are spotted on their approach to the far shore. Weapons, tools, and a five day supply of food and water are also carried on board by the crews. For them, each journey across the Gulf of Aden also carries a risk, and so they spend the previous days in Bossaso with the smugglers getting drunk, chewing qat, smoking hashish and in bed with their wives or prostitutes. By the time they are ready to depart, most are high and edgy, wielding their power with great bravado in front of the terrified tahrib whose lives are at their mercy.

Above right

As volleys of gunfire ring out from the water's edge, an Ethiopian refugee runs up a sandbank and into rocks behind the beach at Ras Shimbiro. Hundreds of tahrib waiting to depart are already hiding up in the cliffs, well away from the smugglers and crews who are becoming increasingly violent as night falls.

As a storm sets in during the night, a smuggler's boat becomes beached in rough seas at a remote cove on Somalia's coast. Summoned by bursts of live gunfire, migrants and refugees sleeping in the surrounding mountains are ordered by the armed gangs to help stabilise the stricken vessel that they are waiting to board. Using ropes, they work in chain gangs at gunpoint, pulling hard to tow the boat into fierce incoming waves in an attempt free it from the sands.

One in Twenty

Drenched and covered in sand, bodies slowly crawl up onto the beach from the dark sea. Having been dropped off in the middle of the night far from shore in order to avoid detection, surviving migrants and refugees shiver violently, still choking on seawater and gasping for breath as they make it onto dry land. Weak and disorientated after spending the past two days at sea, small groups huddle together on a remote Yemeni beach, unaware of the corpses that slowly drift in on the tide behind them.

One in twenty of the tahrib who flee from violent conflict, insecurity or dire conditions in Africa's Horn, in the hope of finding a new life in Yemen, will never reach the shores alive. Many will perish in the waters of the Gulf of Aden, as they undertake the treacherous journey in tiny smugglers' boats. Dangerously overcrowded, the unstable vessels are prone to capsizing, and are liable to engine troubles out in the high seas. Migrants and refugees are frequently beaten, murdered or thrown overboard by cruel gangs who use disproportionate violence against the paying passengers they carry. Few on board can swim and yet most are dropped in deep water up to two kilometres from land, as the crews fear being spotted by Yemeni forces and risk coming under fire.

Many of the dead who are washed up along this thousand-kilometre coastline, show the bloody marks of injuries sustained at the hands of the smugglers. Others have simply drowned, unable to make the final stretch of their long and desperate journey. While a small percentage of the deceased found are given impromptu burials in the sands by local fishermen, nobody knows exactly how many more tahrib perish each year during the crossing. Thousands remain unaccounted for.

For the survivors, the few hours spent on the remote beaches and coves can be frightening. While some migrants quickly abscond in the hope of disappearing without trace, the Somalis who are granted 'prima facie' refugee status in Yemen, sit tight in the hope that help will come soon. Cold, wet and exhausted, few have the energy to move far, and some are yet to succumb to their injuries or to dehydration. In this sparsely populated region, it can take hours before rescue arrives, and with two or three boats often dropping their human cargo almost simultaneously along the coast, groups must often spend much of the night at isolated landing sites.

When assistance does come, the migrants and refugees receive fresh drinking water, milk and biscuits from a local NGO to help revive them. There is no medical relief and no means to dry off or keep warm. Startled in the lights of torch beams, most sit shaking or else crowd around the engines of the rescue party's vehicles in order to feel a little heat against their bodies. After the formality of being briefly registered, groups appear as ghost-like figures as they walk up from the shore, to be packed into the back of small trucks for the onward journey along the coast.

Heading to a reception centre, they ride along the newly paved coastal highway. Likely better than any road on which the new arrivals have ever travelled before, the realisation that they are in a new country sets in. Passing through high sand dunes that hug the sea at every twist and turn, most spend their time in the truck gazing out across the flat expanse of sea over which they have just come. Encountering uniformed armed Yemeni soldiers at the checkpoints en-route, the migrants and refugees duck down nervously -

having become wise to similar scenarios in Somalia, but now unsure of the protocol, there is a sense of overwhelming relief as they are allowed to continue.

Depending on where the migrants and refugees have landed, it can take anything between one and four hours to reach the UNHCR run centre at Mayfa'ah, or its newer partner camp in the east at Ahwar. Both located on the edge of scruffy inland towns, the small fenced-off reception centres provide a temporary resting place for the traumatised immigrants, who badly need to recuperate after their gruelling journey. On arrival, those in serious need of medical attention will be rushed to the clinics, while doctors and nurses ensure that everybody else receives a check-up, dishing out rehydration salts and patching up cuts and bruises. An initial distribution provides all who pass through here with new clothes, flip-flops and a small hygiene kit. Given a mattress and a blanket each for the duration of their stay, the entrants separate out into the male and female sectors, seeking out shelter in the small breezeblock huts or in tents. Most just collapse with exhaustion; it will be their first comfortable sleep in a long time.

During the two or three day stay, the new arrivals will be briefed in groups as to their new status as refugees or asylum seekers, and given advice about what they can now expect as their new lives in Yemen begin. In addition, each will be called forward by UNHCR staff for individual interviews, where their names and backgrounds are filed, and notes recorded about the journey they have just undertaken. For many, the procedure acts as therapy. They break down upon recalling the trauma they have gone through, the scenes of brutality they have witnessed, and the friends and family now left far behind them.

For the most part, nobody moves far from their mattresses. Slowly regaining their strength through rest and cooked food, some of the refugees and migrants will begin to try and call ahead to family members and contacts with whom they hope to settle, or seek advice from. Otherwise, time spent at the reception centres revolves around the call to prayer and naps. After this brief interim, the next stage of their journey begins.

Right and following pages
Having arrived in the middle of the night following a
fifty-seven hour long voyage from Somalia, dawn breaks
over a group of Ethiopian migrants and refugees at a
sandy beach, near Bir Ali on Yemen's southeastern coast.
A pair of tiny fishing boats sailing close together brought
a total of two hundred and fifty-three tahrib within sight
of land, but coming under fire from Yemeni soldiers,
quickly turned around and headed back out into deep
waters. Returning the following night for a second
attempt, smugglers demanded extra money from
passengers if they wanted to be dropped closer to shore.
Despite protesting at being unable to swim, most were
thrown overboard two kilometres out at sea. At least
thirty passengers are estimated to have drowned; only
twenty-three of the bodies were ever found.
Separated by nationality on arrival, the Somalis were first
counted and then taken away for processing at a nearby
reception centre, just a couple of hours after setting foot
on the beach. The Ethiopians who remain behind have
not been so lucky. Despite being severely traumatised
and dehydrated, soldiers have detained the exhausted
group, fearing that unlike the Somalis who have the
automatic right to remain in Yemen as refugees, they
might try to escape.
It took fifteen hours before they were finally allowed to
proceed to the centre and receive the water, food and
medical attention they so badly needed. Most haven't
eaten or had access to drinking water for a long time now,
having spent days waiting to depart from the Somali
beaches. Others are just in a state of shock. Having been
beaten and robbed by smugglers during the voyage, they
must now proceed on their journey into Yemen knowing
that their friends and relatives are unaccounted for.

The survivors from a group of newly arrived migrants and refugees spend their first night on Yemeni soil in the pitch black at a beach near Bir Ali.

Soaking wet and covered in sand, groups of newly arrived Somali migrants huddle together on the beach at Fuwwah as they try to keep warm. Landing in the early hours of the morning after crossing the Gulf of Aden in tiny boats operated by smugglers, most are tired and disorientated after the dangerous two day voyage. One of three boatloads of migrants and refugees that left Somalia together, the group lost sight of the others as high waves almost overwhelmed them during a patch of bad weather. Assumed to have been lost at sea, one of the boats never arrived in Yemen.

Having just spent the last twenty-eight hours at sea on the crossing from Somalia, exhausted groups of men and women crouch on Hamarah Beach in the middle of the night. Hidden behind dunes in a pitch black deserted rocky cove on Yemen's southern coast, it took a further three hours before fishermen eventually located the refugees.

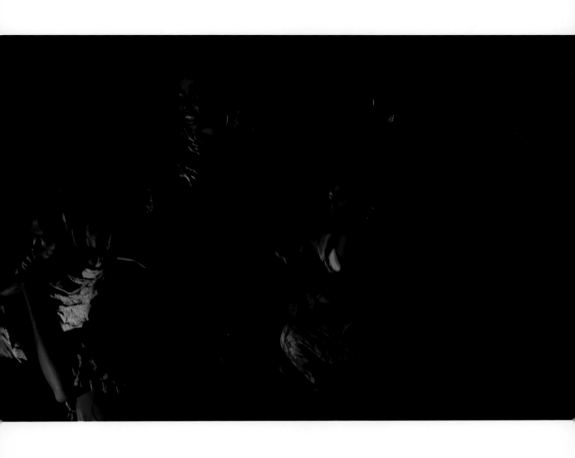

Following pages

Having paid a million shillings each, for these survivors on a beach near Bir Ali, the realisation of just what a gamble they have taken with their own destinies hits home. Weak and barely able to move, hours after landing many still lie with their faces half buried in the sand, still coughing after having swallowed so much sea water. Many sit weeping, having spent the night looking for lost relatives, or simply in shock at the mortality that surrounds them.

A torch illuminates the face of a distressed refugee after a boatload of Somali men and women were discovered on a secluded beach near Hamarah, on Yemen's southeastern sea board. Discovered by a local police patrol in the early hours of the morning, the dishevelled group were sitting among rocks, shivering and in silence. Having been tied up on board the tiny boat that had carried them across the Gulf of Aden, the voyagers have gone for two days without sleep. Checked over one by one by the police officers, their lights revealed that many had sustained beatings from the smugglers paid to help them escape.

Above left
A torch beam casts light on a lone woman sitting shaking and terrified under the cliffs of Burum Beach. High winds and waves have left this sodden group of arrivals freezing after they had to wade ashore from smugglers' boats.

Below left
On the stony ground at Burum Beach, sixty year old Faduma Esse Hassan is discovered lying alone halfway up the shore. Barely conscious and incredibly weak after wading through the sea, she clasps a doctor's letter written in English confirming she is diabetic.

Crouching under black volcanic cliffs in a rocky cove, it took more than four hours for this group of Somali refugees to be discovered after landing on a secluded beach in the dead of night. Escorted by authorities to a nearby police station at Burum, the new arrivals were then contained on the road outside until proper assistance arrived. Provided with milk and biscuits to sustain them, they were subsequently taken by truck to a UNHCR run reception centre.

Previous pages
Illuminated by torchlight, the dead body of a man is discovered in shallow water at Al-Baida Beach. Brutal marks around his face reveal that he had sustained a heavy beating prior to being thrown into the sea. One of a group of three hundred and sixty five migrants and refugees to have arrived that night on two smugglers' boats, survivors witnessed passengers being pummelled with rifle butts and knives as they protested at being dropped far from land. In the dark sea, many succumbed to the water, disorientated and unable to swim. By morning, a total of thirty-four bodies were found at Al-Baida; either drowned or killed at the hands of the smugglers.

Left
Having been washed ashore with the morning tide, a row of corpses line Al-Baida Beach at dawn. Hauled from the water by fellow voyagers, a total of thirty-four bodies were found at sunrise as they slowly drifted inland.
Just one week after an almost identical tragedy saw thirty dead on a nearby beach, Somali smugglers continue to drop migrants and refugees out at sea without regard for life, rather than come close to shore and risk detection.

Beaten to death, the bloody bodies of individuals killed at the hands of smugglers lie washed up on the white sands of Al-Baida Beach. Brought ashore by the tide hours after their deaths, the corpses of those murdered before they entered the water are easy to distinguish. Unlike the countless migrants and refugees who drown so close to the end of their dangerous voyage, there are no traces of foaming salt water around their mouths, only the vicious marks left by rifle butts, sticks and hammers. Despite being renowned for their brutality, those desperate to escape Africa's Horn easily disregard the stories they have heard about the smuggling gangs, thinking only of the better life they hope to find. The beaches of southern Yemen have become graves for thousands of unidentified migrants and refugees. Until a shallow hole in the sand can be dug for these victims, crabs will move in to take their share as they spend the next few hours feasting on the soft tissues.

Following pages
As the waters recede on the twenty-kilometre stretch of beach that runs either side of Luhibila, bodies buried by the tide are revealed under the sands. Testimonies from surviving migrants and refugees that arrived in the same group, tell of leaving Somalia in three tiny fishing boats. Carrying over one hundred and twenty passengers each, one of the vessels has been missing at sea for the last three days. Little hope can be held out now for survivors. Ten further corpses of young men and women were discovered later that evening washed up along the same stretch of coast. As the stiff bodies lay in a row with their eyes open turned to the sky, local fishermen covered the faces of the victims with their veils and macawiis as a mark of respect. Three dead Ethiopian women were left untouched.

Following the southern seaboard for more than six hundred kilometres, Yemen's coastal highway hugs the Gulf of Aden at every twist and turn. There is little traffic to be stopped at the sleepy checkpoints along the route. Aside from the gas plant at Balhaf and a couple of military bases, the only landmarks are small fishing villages. East of Aden, the atmosphere in the tribal provinces of Abyan, Shabwa and Hadramout can be tense. Men armed with Kalashnikovs, Uzis, pistols and grenades openly walk the streets. Terrorist attacks targeting institutions such as police stations and schools have taken place, and the government does not exercise the control it would wish for beyond the roads. Reputedly a hide out for Al-Qaeda linked insurgents, the area holds a strong draw for militants, arms traffickers and smugglers.

Left
Crowded together, encampments of wooden fishermen's shacks appear like a small shantytown on the sweeping bay at Burum village.

Centre
Almost hugging the sea, the coastal highway runs alongside a rocky beach near the village of Mayfa'ah Hagar.

Right
A long straight stretch of Yemen's southern coast road rolls between sand and scrub-covered lava fields close to the liquefied natural gas plant at Balhaf.

Following up reports of recently disembarked migrants and refugees that often come from local fishermen, a two or three man team from NGO Society for Humanitarian Solidarity (SHS) will set out to verify sightings and provide basic assistance. Based in villages along the length of Yemen's southern shoreline, and on standby twenty-four hours a day, the teams usually respond to numerous calls every week. With the smugglers' boats often arriving en-masse when the weather is good, the alerts can come several times in a night. With each unit covering hundreds of kilometres of coast, it can sometimes take hours to reach and locate the often remote drop-off points. When SHS do arrive, they provide fresh drinking water, milk and biscuits to the weary and dehydrated arrivals, before tallying numbers and nationalities. Coordinating with UNHCR, trucks are then sent in order to transfer new arrivals to a dedicated reception centre at Mayfa'ah.

For the majority of Somalis and Ethiopians arriving in Yemen, SHS are the first people they encounter, and despite the reassurances, the onward drive to Mayfa'ah can be disorientating. Huddled in the back of a tightly packed truck, passing Arabic-speaking men in uniform at checkpoints on a smooth metalled road, most of the passengers spend the entire journey looking back out across the Gulf of Aden, keeping their eyes fixed on the horizon. They have come a long way, and have survived thus far. For now though, they have no idea where they are headed.

Having arrived with the bright lights of the port city of Mukalla in their sights, a boatload of Somali refugees were quickly spotted by police and transferred to a local station. Taking frivolous risks, smugglers have been taunting Yemeni authorities by dumping their human cargo on beaches just a few kilometres away from the urban centre.

Soaked through with seawater, a group of more than one hundred Somalis have been permitted to use the washrooms at the police station. Bathing and rinsing out their clothes, one by one they hang them on a long line to dry. As the officers try to glean information, much of the group crouch half-dressed in silence, unsure what will happen to them next. Within a few hours, a bus and truck will come to transport the latest new arrivals nearly two hundred kilometres along the coast to a transit centre at Mayfa'ah. It will be an anxious journey for them.

Arriving in the early hours of the morning at the UNHCR run Mayfa'ah Reception Centre, exhausted migrants and refugees carry mattresses as they search for a resting place in the partitioned male and female areas.

Following a forty-eight hour journey on boats from Somalia, the sheer tiredness on their faces is all too apparent. Women struggle to lift the heavy mattresses and bedding, as their children barely keep up behind them. The men wander off in the opposite direction, bleary-eyed and in silence. With several boatloads having arrived in the last few days, there is little room to lie down in the breezeblock bungalows. After going from door to door searching for space, many simply drop to the ground outside. When they wake up to their first morning in Yemen, they will be given tea and porridge, clean clothes and have their first bath in a few days. The most needed thing right now though is sleep.

Following pages
Queuing along a wire fence, women form a long line as they wait to receive a cooked dinner ration of tea, rice and a little fish, from a busy kitchen at the Mayfa'ah Reception Centre. Exhausted after their long journeys, over the coming two or three days in the transit centre, the temporary residents will receive a cooked breakfast, lunch and dinner as they recover their strength.

Having been transferred from distant beaches along the Yemeni coast, Somali refugees disembark from trucks at the Mayfa'ah Reception Centre. Women and children sit on plastic sheeting laid out just inside the gates; the much larger group of men squeeze into a fenced-off covered waiting area, better designed for keeping a small herd of goats out of the sun. Being nearly four o'clock in the morning, the arrivals will be only briefly registered for now, as staff take just names and nationalities. The nervous group make progress slow, and as they wait patiently, handfuls disappear off for a few minutes to an adjacent makeshift mosque, to say prayers and give thanks to God. Once the process is complete, individuals will be given a mattress and bedding as they finally lay down to a restful sleep. It has taken weeks to get this far and most are on the brink of collapse.

Tomorrow the new arrivals will re-group for a talk. They will be informed of regulations at
the centre, told what to expect next and how to claim official refugee status. In addition they
will be given an informal introduction to Yemeni customs, that warns them about the risk of
robbery and informs them of social conventions - the advice goes even so far as to suggest that
they don't urinate on a stranger's wall. At the end of it all, each will be interviewed and their
details properly logged. They are then free to spend the next few days recuperating.
Their journey isn't over yet, but it is nearing its end.

During their short stay in transit at Mayfa'ah, the newly arrived will spend the majority of their time resting. Their escape from the Horn of Africa has been a long and harrowing journey and they badly need the few days to convalesce. Comprising of small cell-like whitewashed bungalows arranged around two squares, there is little to do in the small reception centre, located in the back streets of a scruffy inland town.

A clinic treats the sick, injured and dehydrated, while the office provides a focal point where the residents gather, relating their experiences to staff in almost informal therapy sessions. A few sit under a sunshade doing their laundry, or venture out to see what is on sale in the local shops, otherwise life here revolves around meal and prayer times.

In a few days they will be transported to the more permanent camp at Al-Kharaz where they will be given the choice to settle, or to move on again with new refugee papers. Either way, it will finally be the start of their new lives.

Previous pages
Men gather for Maghrib prayers at one of four mosques in the Mayfa'ah reception centre.
Designated by low concrete walls in the camp's sleeping areas, prayers at the mosque define
the rhythm of the day as the new arrivals' journeys come to a brief standstill.

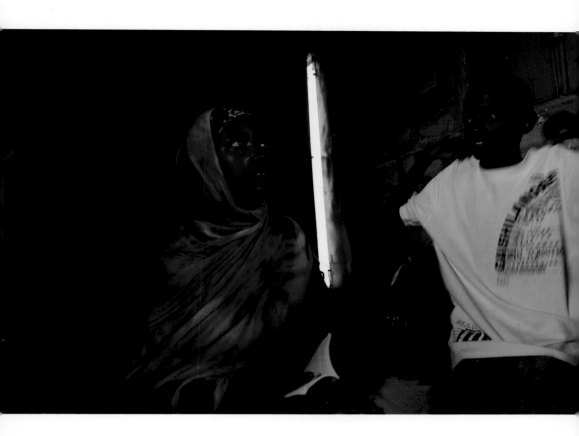

Above

Sitting in one of the women's bungalows at the Mayfa'ah transit centre, a boy trying on a new donated T-shirt looks over at a teenage girl reading a copy of the Qur'an, brought from home in Mogadishu. She has carried the small holy book with her throughout her long journey from Somalia. Arriving in Yemen with no otherworldly possessions, it is her only keepsake.

Following page, from top to bottom

As day breaks, a refugee sleeps wrapped in a blanket on the ground in one of the camp's open-air mosques.

A newly arrived refugee waits in a shaded area outside the UNHCR registration office.

Men do their laundry against the fenced-off rocky backdrop of Yemen's Shabwa province.

Resting out of the hot sun in one of the Mayfa'ah Reception Centre's breezeblock bungalows, newly arrived Somali refugee Aweis Ahmed Mohamed kneels down on his mattress in prayer. A tailor from the war-torn Medina area in Mogadishu, the father of three has left behind his family in search of finding a more secure life in Yemen. Planning to join his brother Ibrahim who works washing cars in Aden's Basatine slum, his dream was for his family to follow once he had established himself. Now after the journey he's not so sure. Feeling broken and traumatised, Aweis was robbed of all his money and possessions by the smuggling gang he had put his trust in, and left terrified after the crossing made on a tiny vessel that was barely sea-worthy. "I don't think there is a chance anymore. I really wouldn't want my wife and children to travel here on these boats".

Welcome to Kharaz

It can take up to ten hours to travel along the southern coast in trucks that depart from the reception centres. Passing through the large modern port city of Aden, most of the migrants and refugees on board will be overwhelmed by the street and traffic lights, wide, paved roads, shopping centres and bustling commerce, the likes of which they have never seen before. The journey at last signals that they are now in a new country and in a new continent.

East of Aden, it takes just another two hours along the desert highway that stretches to Saudi Arabia before they reach the turn-off to a bumpy unpaved road that will lead them to Yemen's only refugee camp. Dropped off outside a walled compound on the edge of this remote outpost, a blue painted sign reading, "You are welcome to UNHCR Kharaz" greets the new arrivals. For the majority of refugees and asylum seekers, Al-Kharaz is where they will finally collect their identity papers confirming their refugee status or leave to remain in Yemen.

Their numbers swelled in recent times, as migrants and refugees land at Dhubab on Yemen's western seaboard via new smuggling routes from Djibouti, hundreds are dropped outside the camp's offices every week. It can take some time for the NGOs based at Al-Kharaz to process the large groups, and so for now, the new arrivals are escorted to a designated tented area of the camp until being called forward for registration.

A long walk from the welcome point takes them through the centre of this sprawling camp. Isolated in a rocky, dusty desert far from any settled areas, the light and heat can be fierce. Relocated successively over the years since the outbreak of Somalia's civil war, the Yemeni government most recently established the refugee camp at the former military base of Al-Kharaz in 2000, pushing the residents further from their points of arrival, firmly out of sight into this bleak inhospitable place. Home to 17,000 largely Somali refugees, the current camp extends over several square kilometres around the abandoned facility.

Centred on a wide stony street of mosques, tea stalls and shops selling basic commodities, backhandedly referred to as "Aden Mall", the camp extends out in all directions. Long-term inhabitants are housed in zones of tiny numbered breezeblock bungalows, each separated by a purda of hedges made of thorns and scrub. Inside the huts there are few comforts, while the yards contain hand-built mud latrines and cooking areas, and often a few precious chickens or goats. On the periphery, sprawling encampments of temporary shelters built from sticks, cardboard, sheets and found materials are a mirror of the decrepit bush camps that are home to so many displaced in Somalia. It can take years for the residents of these tattered windblown settlements to be allocated more permanent homes despite continued construction efforts.

Monthly food and aid distributions provide only the most basic of necessities to survive, and with scant cooking fuel, few residents eat more than a couple of meagre meals of bread, tea and pulses a day. Comprised largely of vulnerable individuals, children and women widowed by war or during the escape from Somalia, nearly all of the population depends solely on the assistance provided by UNHCR. Having run from conflict and suffering at home, for the refugees that eke out a life here, Al-Kharaz is a woeful escape.

For the new arrivals coming to Yemen with high expectations, the bleakness and abjection of Al-Kharaz can seem a bitter blow. Most have already sketched out other plans to seek job opportunities in the cities, or to track down friends and relatives settled elsewhere, but had at least presumed that there would be a better alternative to the equally impoverished camps back home. After the formalities of form filling, interviews and having their photographs taken, only the truly desperate stay on.

For the first few days, most of the disenfranchised newcomers make for the small telephone kiosks and money transfer offices in the camp that have come to typify each stage of the long journey. In this distant setting, they must first make plans to migrate from Al-Kharaz to the hub of Aden. Four-wheel drive vehicles run by locals ply the route, but the prices charged are high, and once again days can be spent waiting for funds to be sent from home. Scraping together the little money they have, or begging the vendors for credit, the newly arrived refugees place their first overseas calls from Yemen. Talking emotionally to friends and family who are overwhelmed just to hear that their loved ones are alive, pledges from home are made to seek out hawala bureaus so that the immigrants' journeys can draw to a close.

When the new arrivals do move on, there are heart-felt farewells to be said to the fellow tahrib who have become such close friends during the long and perilous journey made together. Leaving behind the vast, impoverished desert settlement of their fellow countrymen and women at Kharaz Camp, they disappear now, as official refugees to the city.

Previous pages
Utterly exhausted, a group of Somali refugees crouch down beneath an illuminated signboard reading, "You are welcome to UNHCR Kharaz". Arriving close to Dhubab on Yemen's western coast in a smuggler's boat that has brought them across the Bab El-Mendab Straits from Djibouti, the stranded group were spotted by military camped on a nearby beach. Transported by truck, the refugees have finally arrived at Yemen's only refugee camp in the early hours of the morning. As staff are alerted, they must sit and wait outside the main gates for now. Once morning comes, they will be called to an office and formerly registered one by one, their cases documented and their photographs taken. Finally, they will be given official status as refugees.

Left
Carrying a walking stick, a Somali elder wearing a macawiis and prayer cap heads back to his home in Kharaz Camp's block fourteen.

Above
At dusk, a newly arrived refugee runs through one of the wide-open spaces in the sprawling camp as he tries to catch up with friends.

245

Having been registered that afternoon, two men hold hands as they venture out to explore the sprawling camp at Al-Kharaz. Heading along the dusty main street lined by ramshackle shops and cafes, they are miles from home but could for all intents and purposes be almost anywhere in Somalia.

Few young men and women who arrive in Yemen will want to take up residence at Al-Kharaz. Rather than settle for a dead-end existence in the isolated desert, they move on soon after receiving their refugee papers and cards. For many, the next step will be finding the fare into Aden. Accessible only by four-wheel drives and with Somalis often banned from travelling on the connecting roads, the Yemeni drivers who run the route steeply overcharge for the journey. Most new arrivals will spend the next few days in the call centres and money transfer offices that dot the camp, begging friends and relatives for extra cash.

Located approximately one hundred and fifty kilometres west of Aden, Al-Kharaz camp has grown from the remnants of a disused military base in a barren, isolated patch of desert. Aside from a few small encampments and villages of pastoralists, there is nothing else for miles around. This hostile, unforgiving environment is far removed from the promised land that many of the refugees have risked their lives for.

Home to more than seventeen thousand, much of the featureless camp is comprised of small numbered breezeblock shelters surrounded by makeshift fences of thorns and sheets. Allocated over the years to long-term and vulnerable refugees, the majority of residents have settled here out of necessity rather than choice and are dependent on the assistance they receive from UNHCR.

On the far periphery of Al-Kharaz, a fenced off tented camp provides
shelter for new arrivals. At times, the pitched tents can be seriously
overcrowded and are unbearably hot as scorching winds blow in from
the surrounding desert. The only respite are the outdoor water taps
where the refugees can regularly be seen cooling themselves off.
Thousands pass through here each year. Most just spend a few days resting
and making plans for the lives that are about to unfold ahead of them.
Looking around, there is little reason to stay put.

For the refugees who do stay put at Al-Kharaz, it might take two or three years to be allocated
a permanent shelter. The waiting list is long and the clusters of accommodation blocks expand
slowly. Leaving behind the tented transit area for new arrivals, they move on to the sprawling
bush camp, that looks almost identical to those many have known in Somalia. Building their
own shelters from found materials, they collect dead wood from the surrounding desert,
covering the crudely constructed structures with old clothes, sheets, cardboard and sacks.
Some move into the skeletal ruins that previous occupants have left behind, reinforcing
the patchwork covers as and when suitable components come their way. Distributions of
non-food items provide residents with pots and pans and a plastic sheet that helps give some
protection from the elements. Monthly rations of rice, flour and pulses provide basic sustenance,
but few can afford to supplement their diet. Far away from home and the outside world, the bush
camp is a stark reminder of how desperate life was, and still is for its inhabitants.

Following pages
Dropped on Yemen's western shores by a wooden smuggler's boat originating in Djibouti, a small group of young refugees arrive at Al-Kharaz after navigating their way through the desert. Walking the fifty kilometres from Dhubab out of sight from the roads, for fear they might be fleeced by bandits or soldiers, they have trekked overnight, reaching the camp in the heavy midday heat. Greeted by police at a small post located near the camp's entrance, the exhausted, hungry group were invited to finish off the lunch of rice and fish that the officers had just tucked into.

Previous pages
Having been registered and interviewed by UNHCR staff at Al-Kharaz,
a sick woman is attended to by a nurse after being referred to the clinic for
medical attention. Providing basic health care for the camp's seventeen
thousand residents and a feeding programme for malnourished children,
two wards treat the seriously ill and those who have sustained injuries
during their journey from Somalia.

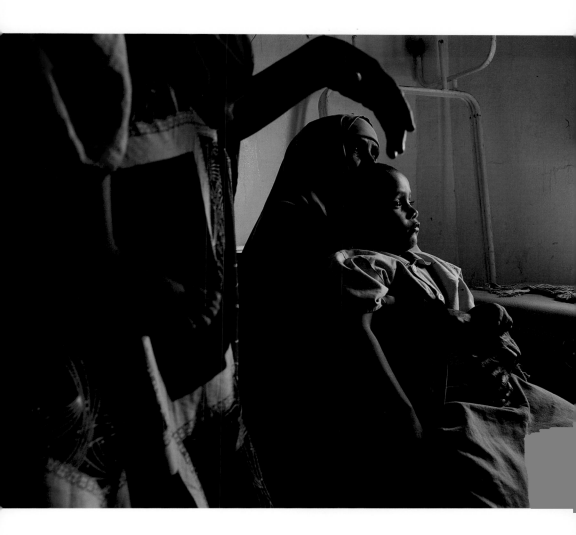

Top left
Clutching her refugee identity card and ration coupons, a woman tries to make her way past police acting as security during a monthly food distribution.

Bottom left
Women are waved back through a doorway as they try to push their way past an agitated crowd in the long wait for monthly food rations.

Above
At the head of the queue, a woman clutching her sick young son on her lap waits to see a doctor in the clinic at Al-Kharaz camp.

Run by the renowned Foors and her twin daughters, the simple thatched Wa'afa Restaurant
has become an institution at Al-Kharaz camp. Coming alone with her children to Yemen at the
outbreak of civil war in Somalia, Foors started out selling plates of food in Yemen's first refugee
camp at Al-Sha'b. As the locations of the camps have changed over the years, she has reopened the
restaurant at each site, as along with thousands of others she was forced to move on.
Cooking, cleaning and serving customers from dawn until dusk each day, she has a hard time
keeping up with the demand for her tasty cheap eats. Lately she has even expanded the restaurant
out back, covering the floor with vinyl so she can seat more diners when the wooden tables and
benches become full. A determined and lively woman, she works hard to support her family in an
environment where few refugees succeed. By lunchtime, the Wa'afa Restaurant is packed. Some
young children are hanging around outside hoping to get some scraps so Foors gives them each a
small bowl of porridge then quickly sits back behind the stove.

Left
Foors's daughter Suad sweeps up after a customer in the back dining room at the Wafa'a Restaurant.

Right
Hanging around the restaurant in search of food scraps, a small girl licks clean a bowl of porridge she has been given.

Run by long-term residents, small grocery stores-come-telephone bureaus and money transfer offices dot the camp at Al-Kharaz. Many young men and women head straight to these call centres on arrival, spending hours as they try again and again to reach family members in Somalia on lines that are frequently down. Most just want to send word back to home that they are alive and in Yemen, while others desperately plead for help and money. Late into the evening, the shops remain packed as the new refugees hold out in last-ditch attempts as the operators keep redialling. When they do get through, there are often tears. Few tell of what they have been through, they are looking ahead now, and wondering what might come next.

The hub of shops and services at Al-Kharaz line a wide dusty street at the heart of the camp that has become jokingly known as "Aden Mall", after the glitzy new shopping centre in the city some three hours away. Here though there are no fancy supermarkets or clothes shops selling imported goods, that remain illusive for the refugees, only small windows cut from wire mesh or corrugated iron serving up basic groceries, sodas and samosas. Kiosks painted with the flags of Somalia and Oromia sell qat and provide shade for a few traders selling vegetables laid out on sacks amid the dirt. Less obvious are the money transfer offices and call centres usually distinguished by a world map or posters of skyscrapers that they have pinned to the walls. Just behind the shops a concrete patch surrounded by barbed wire is home to a morning fish market but out in the open desert it disappears before lunchtime, when the heat becomes intolerable.

In the cool of the evening, Aden Mall comes to life once again with shoppers and men sipping chai at their regular cafes, before heading to the open-air mosque for Maghreb prayers.

Previous pages and above

Coming to Yemen when he was just a baby, fourteen year old Mohamed Noor had already lost one toe after being injured during a firefight, in his home town of Kismayo in southern Somalia. Now along with his six siblings and widowed mother Asri, he lives in a graffiti-covered room of an abandoned military building at the Al-Kharaz camp. Without a father, Mohamed and his family are considered "at risk" and are hoping to be re-settled to a third country; a process that could take years. Having spent almost his whole life growing up in the confines of refugee camps, Mohamed's only escape are his pet birds. He brings them down from the roof to play with when he gets depressed.

Mohamed Noor's sister Mariam prepares food in the shaded kitchen of the family's temporary home, located in a desolate former army barracks on the outskirts of Al-Kharaz.

Old pieces of torn foam and dirty sheets are piled together to form a temporary improvised bed in the corridor of a stone built warehouse at the former military base. A place to sleep here is relative luxury at Al-Kharaz Camp; out of the hot winds and sun, this resting place would be much envied by those sleeping on dirt floors under plastic sheeting or canvas.

Crippled by a paralysing disease since he was a small child, nineteen year old Ismail crawls using flip-flops on his hands, through the tent of his adopted family at Al-Kharaz Camp. Ismail doesn't know the name of the disease he has, his parents only referred to it as the "bad wind".

Managing to survive independently in Mogadishu by running a phone booth, Ismail's condition only made security worse for him. He was constantly harassed by the Al-Shabaab militia and was unable to run when his home came under attack. In one case, incessant heavy fighting around his booth trapped him inside for five days. Saving a little money and with some small donations, Ismail set out for Yemen with a group of friends on a long journey that took him via Galkayo, Hargeysa and Djibouti on three trucks. Finally reaching the tip of the Arabian Peninsula on a smuggler's boat, a young Somali boy carried Ismail ashore on his shoulders.

Although the friends he travelled with have now moved on, an NGO placed Ismail with Mama Amina's family, who have agreed to care for him in their meagre shelter located in Al-Kharaz's bush camp. Amina cooks for him and even collects his bath water as he slowly settles in. Despite now being free from violent conflict, Ismail wishes he could support himself again as he did in Mogadishu. In Yemen though, that can never happen.

From the minority Bantu clan, Bardeen Abdullah Omar and her husband Ali Abdi Saed, escaped Somalia after continued persecution and violent threats against their family. They have since made their home in a room of some abandoned army barracks in the former military base that is now Yemen's only refugee camp. With an eleven month old son, the couple can see no other future for themselves but to eke out an existence in the harsh deserts of southern Yemen. Living amongst a group of fellow clans people they at least feel safe, and Bardeen has started selling vegetables to make the family a little money.

Meanwhile, Ali has been meeting with some of the Bantu elders; they have become proactive and have begun thinking of ways to raise awareness about the squalid conditions they are forced to live in. Unable to return home, the Somali Bantu have been writing letters appealing for resettlement of the two thousand plus refugees they represent in Al-Kharaz. They describe themselves as having been "ethnically cleansed".

Waiting to be registered at the UNHCR office in Al-Kharaz Camp, a young boy wearing a keffiyeh, who has seemingly travelled alone from Somalia, sits half asleep at a table with his head in his hands.

Armed with Kalashnikov rifles, local Yemeni pastoralists stop for tea at a café in
Al-Kharaz Camp as they pass through the country's southern deserts on camels.

Above

Sitting close to the floor on rows of benches without legs, men while away a few hours watching television at a recreation centre in Al-Kharaz Camp. The centre offers adult education, basic skills training such sewing and barbering classes, a gym and a dedicated room where women can meet. Mostly though, it serves as an escape from the heat, and a place to relax.

Right

Resting with his face in his hands, nine year old orphan Said Sallah lies on a mattress watching television at the back of his adopted family's shop. Said's parents lost their lives as they neared the end of the family's long journey to Yemen; they are assumed to have drowned. Arriving alone at Al-Kharaz just over a year ago, an NGO found a family willing to adopt Said. Sala and his wife Johara run a shop in the camp and unable to have children of their own, enthusiastically welcomed the boy that they now call their son. Said sometimes seems distant and is very quiet for his age; they hope that soon he might be a little more talkative.

Following pages
Heading towards one of Al-Kharaz camp's accommodation blocks at sundown, a woman is helped out by her son and daughter as they carry home pots, pans and plastic sheeting following a distribution of non-food items.
Women make up more than half the heads of families in Al-Kharaz. Separated from their husbands through conflict and insecurity, the camp has become a place of exile for thousands of single mothers. Almost all are completely reliant on the rations and aid they receive but it is barely enough to provide for their children. Having escaped from Somalia, their relinquished destinies now lie in this forsaken desert internment.

The Cowboys of Eden

Named after the fabled garden, the city of Aden is the supposed paradise that so many of the tahrib have dreamed of since the outset of their journeys. For tens of thousands of refugees who land on Yemen's shores each year, it is the end of the road. A second generation of Somalis have taken root here, largely concentrated around the outlying ghetto of Basatine, in an area that has over the years become known as "Little Mogadishu".

Long-term residents in Basatine have a name for those fresh off the boats; they call them *lo jire*, meaning cowboys, owing mainly to the swagger with which they walk as they set foot in their aspired "Eden". Transport from the desert camp at Al-Kharaz drops them directly to the ever-chaotic noisy bus and taxi stands at the heart of the ghetto. In this dusty, rubbish strewn square with its noisy throng of touts, qat sellers and market traders all of Somali descent; they have finally made it.

Disorientated and overwhelmed, the cowboys hide their trepidation as they venture out. Free to wander the streets of Yemen for the first time since landing, they are brimming with enthusiasm. Most head straight to the makeshift cafes and restaurants adjacent to the bus parks where groups of unemployed refugees spend their days drinking tea, chatting or watching television under tattered canvas awnings. Named after regions of Somalia, their walls are decorated with posters and maps from back home and once inside these shelters, the feeling is of a town having merely been transported across the gulf. In between serving up plates of watery spaghetti and pouring thermos flasks of green chai, the owners and vendors here are predisposed to dishing out advice to the newcomers on an almost daily basis; they have been here for years and know almost every face and family in Basatine.

Many of the new arrivals come to Aden seeking out relatives or old friends and acquaintances. Others bring the carefully noted names and telephone numbers kept with them in the tiny address books that they have treasured since leaving home in the hope of finding the contacts within. For some, it is a simple case of asking a few questions or picking up directions in order to locate those they are in search of. Starting their lives afresh, some ask about job opportunities but are quickly disheartened to learn that there are few going, and life in Aden is far harder than the easy future conjured up by the smugglers. Restricted as refugees to take on formal employment, the prospects for the young and able here are little more than hand to mouth work labouring, or else joining the throngs of Somalis washing cars or collecting scrap on the city's streets. Women can do little more than go begging or seek underpaid jobs as servants behind closed doors. For now though, the priority for the new arrivals is to find shelter and somewhere to spend their first nights.

Crudely constructed from corrugated iron and plywood sheeting, the seriously overcrowded squats that line the dirty alleyways radiating out from Basatine's main square are an expensive option. Landowners charge extortionately high rents for the dishevelled properties, forcing up to three families or a dozen individuals to share one cramped partitioned room. Toilets are allotted between the residents of surrounding shacks and even water must be bought to order, delivered to the households by donkey or camel carts that navigate the lanes. As thousands more new arrivals descend on the ghetto each year, competition for space among the established community becomes even tougher and it can be hard to find a place here to call home.

Fuelled by the economy of immigration the telephone kiosks, money changers and hawala bureaus, denoted by Somali shillings taped up outside tin shacks, attract those who might still be able to receive assistance from home. With their family's generosity exhausted, many newcomers however spend their initial time in Basatine simply walking the congested streets, or hanging around in shaded areas, before bedding down in the open around the bus and taxi stands where they first alighted. In order to eat they are reduced to asking for zakat, an Islamic form of charitable donation, often from other impoverished refugees who recognise their plight.

Outwardly vulnerable, the disenfranchised, women and unaccompanied minors easily fall prey to the offers of food and shelter that come from syndicates of human traffickers, whose main income stems from those with nowhere else to turn. With clandestine bases dotted around the slum's back alleys, they offer a place to rest in lieu of the fare for the overland journey to Saudi Arabia. Tempted by the promises of secure jobs and a better life than the one they are confronted with in Yemen, a bond with the traffickers can seem like their best chance. Stuck in a poverty trap, few of the new arrivals who camp out in the covert doss houses will ever be able to pay even the cheapest fares on offer to the border, or repay the debt for their lodgings. Their fate now lies in the hands of merciless gangs who will most likely seek to traffic them to the Kingdom or elsewhere, where they risk effectively becoming enslaved or otherwise abused.

For the cowboys that do settle down to endure a future in the ghetto of Basatine, daily life is harsh and unforgiving, offering few prospects. Far from home, they have swapped insecurity for instability in a place that is a million miles away from their dreams.

286

Bright lights and modern buildings surround the port
area of Ma'alla in downtown Aden.